Understanding

REITs

and

Real Estate

Stocks

REITs-Atlas

List of Symbols
Description, opportunities and risks

1st edition | July 2020

Copyright © 2020 REITs-Atlas

Layout: REITs-Atlas

Cover Design: HB Digital Labs

Cover Picture: Petr Kratochvil

ISBN: XXXX

Reits.atlas@gmail.com

Inhaltsverzeichnis

1   List of Symbols

Disagio: The book value of a REIT's equity is the sum of its assets divided by the number of shares issued. However, the share price results from supply and demand. It fluctuates around the book value per share, but can also move away from it.

If the share price is below the book value, one speaks of a disagio. If a REIT is quoted at a discount, you can expect price recovery potential here if the price approaches the book value again. However, a discount usually has a reason so the exchange participants expect a crisis or worse business conditions and price them in at the stock exchange price.

Agio: If the share price is above the book value, this is called an agio. If a REIT is listed on an agio, there is a risk of a price decline or stagnation if the stock price reduces the overvaluation compared to the book value. There is also a reason for a premium. It is often a REIT with very positive future expectations, so future profits or growth are already priced into the stock price.

Heavyweight: For REITs marked with the symbol for Heavyweights are companies with a market cap of over USD 10 billion. The size is not a mandatory quality feature for a REIT, but REITs can only be achieved through years of good management to grow to such a size. Mostly this size is the dominant player and luminary in the respective category, in which most market participants also invest. However, it is much more important that a REIT with a large market capitalization is traded on the stock exchange much more frequently and more liquidly. With this size, you can expect high liquidity, low bid-ask spreads, high transparency, high observation by analysts and institutional investors as investors. In addition, this category of REITs will be more likely to be traded by standard brokers with a low international focus.

Lightweight: For REITs that have the symbol for Lightweights marked, these are companies with a market capitalization of less than USD 1 billion. In return for the heavyweights, you have to expect less liquidity, transparency and little coverage by analysts. Also, these companies may not be available from every broker or bank, or only at increased order fees.

However, the small size has a positive effect if a REIT flies "under the radar" of analysts and investors and they have not yet recognized its potential. Since market inefficiencies can occur with small market capitalization, you can find bargains on this scale.

Sustainable REITs: The symbol for sustainability becomes awarded if a REIT has been noticed positively for sustainable investments. Sustainability is defined here according to the ESG criteria ("Environment, Social, Governance"). Examples of positive behavior on these three Criteria can be a high proportion of green electricity, special consideration for the environment and building materials during construction, protection of living space for endangered animal species, etc. While some industries are generally unsuitable for this symbol (e.g., oil pipelines), other industries (e.g., forest properties) are predestined for this labeling.

REITs often advertise their sustainability with awards and certificates or are positively mentioned in the media.

Shares without REITs status: The focus of the in Companies covered in this book are REITs that enjoy all legal and tax benefits for this legal form. Basically, however, REITs are completely normal stock corporations, which have only committed themselves to one property focus and requirements for distribution. Real estate stocks that do not comply with these guidelines do not enjoy the tax benefits of a REIT. All profits are taxed normally, as with all other companies. But they are more free toward their business activities. Such companies may still be mentioned in this book if you take an investment approach very similar to the REITs.

Hand-Picked: Hand-Picked REITs are choosen for a characteristic or a business model of a REIT that differs from other REITs and the broad mainstream in its category. This symbol identifies rather unknown but interesting REITs. The label "hand-picked" indicates REITs that are suitable for diversification. "Hand-Picked" REITs can qualify as such because they differ fundamentally from other REITs, but also if they pursue a positive business model within a very comparable category or simply because they have so far been neglected by most analysts and investors. As niche players they can be seen as hidden pearls. This can apply to individual REITs as well as to entire, previously ignored categories.

The symbol "hand-picked" is not a recommendation to buy. However, it indicates REITs that are worth researching more closely.

List of Symbols
Description, opportunities and risks

Rating: A rating, as far as publicly available, follows the classification of the rating agency S&P. It is possible that not all REITs are rated or accessible or only from different agencies with different evaluation criteria or classifications. Rating information is only a rough overview of a company. Further research, analysis and review of the rating and the evaluation criteria must follow by the investor.

Rating information is provided using the following system in descending creditworthiness:

AAA, AA+, AA, AA-, A+, A, A -, BBB +, BBB, BBB-, BB+, BB, BB-, B+, B, B-, CCC+, CCC , CCC-, D.

Dividend frequency: This symbol represents the payment method. There are annual, quarterly, semi-annual and monthly payers. Helped by the symbol you can quickly see whether a dividend will be paid "4x" or "1x" per year.

Diversified: Based on the available Data, REITs are flagged if they are very diversified in their portfolio, e.g., are widely spread across several industries, regions, tenants or even a very large number of properties. A high level of diversification is generally seen as a positive criterion because it minimizes cluster risks.

Focused: The characteristic "focused" is selected, if the business activity is limited to a very narrow niche/business area or the REIT is very small and has only a few rental properties. Focusing on one or very few tenants would also lead to this feature. Focus manifests itself as a positive investment criterion if you add a focused REIT as an admixture

8

to an already broadly diversified portfolio. A concentration of the portfolio in the sense of a cluster risk would count as a negative investment criterion with a focused REIT compared to a diversified one.

Tripple-Net lessor: This symbol indicates REITs, whose business model is largely based on triple net rental agreements (also called NNN). With the triple net method, even more maintenance costs of a building are passed on to the tenant than with normal contracts, e.g., Insurance costs, property tax, etc.

With this method, the basic rent for the REIT is lower, but it is even more stable and predictable. The REIT has even less administration and bookkeeping effort and can manage rental income more efficiently because it hardly needs any employees.

Currency Safe: This symbol identifies all REITs who balance in USD or are based in the United States. As a result, investing in such a REIT involves less currency risk. However, it is still possible that a USD-based REIT owns property in another currency country or concludes rental contracts in foreign currencies.

Foreign currency: This symbol identifies all REITs that are quoted in a currency other than USD. For an investor, these REITs involve currency fluctuations. This can be a risk, but it can also offer opportunities if an appreciation occurs. In any case, the complexity of assessing the value of a REIT increases. However, REITs in foreign currencies can also have positive effects on the diversification of a portfolio.

List of Symbols
Description, opportunities and risks

Categories: The category symbols are based on the division of the categories in the following chapters. These symbols make it easy to see what a REIT is doing. Several symbols per REIT are also possible.

Lodging	**Self-Storage**
Residential	**Prisons**
Student Housing	**Timberland**
Office	**Infrastructure**
Health Care	**Entertainment**
Einzelhandel	**Diversified**
Industrial	**Ground Lease**
Datacenters	**Advertisement**
	Mortgage-REITs

Country of origin: The respective symbol shows the origin of the country and thus the tax and legal handling

10

as a REIT. The location of the investments can deviate from this and be distributed all over the world. In addition, a map in the data sheet of each REIT shows the most important investment regions.

USA		Australia	
Germany		Asia	
Great Britain		Canada	

2   Strategy portfolios:

All REITs in this book are assigned to at least one strategy portfolio based on the following criteria, if possible. But some REITs do not have any properties to be assigned to one of the sample depots. The strategy portfolios provide a rough overview of the suitability of a REIT in relation to the direction and strategy of an investor. A distinction is made between the strategies "diversification", "security" and "return". This assignment is not a recommendation or investment advice. However, it identifies REITs so a reader can see at a glance which REITs might be of interest to his strategy. On this basis, he can analyze them in more detail.

Stability ✅ **Strategy portfolio "Stability":** REITs are
Diversification ✅ assigned to the strategy portfolio
Yield ✅

Strategy portfolios:
Description, opportunities and risks

"Stability" if they meet at least one of these criteria:

A REIT's rating is investment grade (better than BBB-). The market capitalization of a REIT is more than USD 10 billion. The REIT belongs to the group of so-called "dividend aristocrats". The REIT is a member of the S&P 500 stock exchange index. The REIT has an inherently very stable business model (forest, arable land or ground lease). The REIT has a low debt ratio of less than 30%. The REIT is quoted in USD and is, therefore, not subject to currency fluctuations.

A REIT from the "Stability" strategy portfolio is suitable for investors who prefer the preservation of value and the stability of their investment. You consider a REIT more like a bond with stable and predictable distributions and does not have to fear major price fluctuations.

Stability ⊘
Diversification ⊘
Yield ✅

Strategy portfolio "Yield": REITs are assigned to the strategy portfolio "Yield" if they meet at least one of these criteria:

The dividend yield of the REIT is higher than 5% p.a. (The dividend yield at the time of the publication of this book will change later, but the rough division into REITs with high or low returns can still be seen from this). The business model of the REIT is characterized by strong growth rates (e.g., radio masts or data centers) and a price increase may be expected (momentum). The REIT is a mortgage REIT that traditionally has a very high dividend yield.

A REIT from the "Return" strategy portfolio is suitable for investors who place higher weighting on price gains and high dividends.

Stability ✓ **Strategy portfolio "Diversification":**
Diversification ✓ REITs are assigned to the strategy
Yield ✓ portfolio "Diversification" if they meet
at least one of these criteria:

The REIT pursues an exceptional business model very different from that of other REITs (either general or within a category). The REIT comes from a country other than the USA. The REIT's investments are widely spread regionally. The REIT's investments are spread across several industries or very broad tenant groups.

A REIT from the "Diversification" strategy portfolio is suitable for investors who want to avoid cluster risks through high diversification. Both focused and diversified REITs can be suitable for diversification. With focused REITs, you can achieve more diversity and independence in your depot as an admixture.

3   What are REITs?

3.1   Description, opportunities and risks

REITs are "Real Estate Investment Trusts", which translates to "real estate investment companies". REITs are listed capital gathering points that invest investors' money in real estate. They are active in the fields of development, administration and management of real estate, real estate or mortgages.

REITs are normal stock corporations with an investment focus on real estate. They get their separate legal form as REIT by following country-specific requirements. As a result, they enjoy attractive tax breaks in over 40 countries. The most common conditions for REIT status are to distribute most of the profit generated from real estate (usually at least 90%) and the almost complete investment focus on real estate. In these cases, special laws do not result in taxes at the company level. For this reason, REITs generally have very high payouts compared to other stocks.

All known REITs together manage more than $ 3 trillion worldwide. There are approximately $ 2 trillion of assets in the United States alone.

The concept of the REITs originated in the USA, from where most and the best-known representatives of the REITs originate. Because of the quarterly dividends that are common in the United States, this payment pattern also occurs in most REITs. However, some REITs even pay a dividend monthly. These monthly payers are marked with the symbol "12x" in the data sheets of the REITs. REITs are, therefore, especially Suitable for investors who prefer a regular dividend as residual income.

The legal form of the REITs and the associated advantages were created to promote housing construction in the USA and to offer private investors the opportunity to participate in the important asset class of real estate with little money. In the USA, in particular, where retirement provision still has to be largely built up privately, REITs have become a very popular asset class. An investment in real estate via REITs involves significantly fewer administrative requirements and costs than a direct real estate investment.

REITs solve the three core problems of directly held real estate:

Illiquidity

self management

little diversification

These three problems are solved by the REITs' asset class, in that real estate is acquired and owned by a capital collector rather than by the investor directly. The collected customer funds generally give REITs access to objects of a special type or location that a retail investor was denied. When investing in REITs, an investor need not worry about buying, maintaining, renting, vacancy or repairing the property. A REIT collects investors' money and enables broad diversification across a variety of investment properties, tenants and regions. Cluster risks can also be avoided. On the other hand, focal points can also be controlled in specific regions or industries by selecting REITs with the appropriate specialization.

The same applies to diversification into tenants, which can manage a capital collecting point much more broadly than one

individual investor. As a lessor of one or only less directly held apartments, you can face considerable financial difficulties due to loss of rent, refusal to pay, legal disputes or vacancy. REITs invest in so many tenants that a single failure hardly diminishes the return.

REITs are already working internally with outside capital to increase the return on equity. Depending on the REIT, this can be done more conservatively or speculatively. In return for a direct real estate investment, an investor cannot leverage a REIT investment by borrowing. However, he also does not have to be liable for loans from the REIT company and can hand over the responsibility to the management. REITs are indebted with an average of 40-60% of total assets and are, therefore, much more reserved and safer than is the case with private financing.

Lease-contracts often provide a rental period of several years and thus create significantly more security and predictability for this period. If a tenant cancels before the end of the rental contract, he is usually always obliged to continue paying the rent or to pay a contractual penalty.

Many REITs are only established as an asset management company. This means that the buildings or the purpose of the building are not operated themselves. All tenant-related work (e.g., with a hotel: hiring staff, cleaning, room service, etc.) is carried out by the tenant. Due to this construction, REITs generally have very little in-house staff, which

works exclusively in the administration of the REIT. As a result, REITs are very effective and could better plan and control costs and risks.

REITs are public companies and are traded on the stock exchange. They have significantly higher liquidity than individual properties, which you can only laboriously buy or sell through a broker or personal negotiations. The purchase of REIT shares is already possible with small amounts. The order fees of a bank are much cheaper than the ancillary purchase costs of a direct property. There you can save thousands of USD for additional costs such as notary and land registry costs, brokerage fees and real estate transfer tax.

If a crisis occurs, REIT shares can easily be sold on the stock exchange. For a direct real estate investment, it could also happen that you cannot find a buyer for a long period. With sales on the stock exchange, however, panic sales by market participants can occur, which drive the prices to a lower level than justified. Especially with very small REITs with little market liquidity, it can happen that you cannot sell at the desired prices. But they can still act in relation to a direct investment and can protect themselves from even greater losses or a total loss. The sale of REIT shares on the stock exchange can be completed in a few minutes, whereas a property sale can take several months to be completed.

In times of high inflation, investments in REITs represent real assets. Inflation means a devaluation of money by making goods to be bought more expensive. Such Goods are also real estate that could increase or retain their value relative to cash in inflation scenarios.

With foreign REITs, the investment is subject to the risk of currency fluctuations. The investment value or stock exchange price in a foreign currency may increase or decrease in relation to your home currency, which means fluctuations in the sales value and the amount of your dividend.

Since REITs are often tax-privileged because certain requirements are met, there is a potential risk in changing the tax regime. A government that abolishes tax benefits can cause a significant deterioration in the profitability of REITs. Likewise, tax advantages in the country of the REIT cannot develop their advantages if you are taxable as an investor in another country. Regarding withholding taxes, it is possible that double taxes on your income may apply. Future legislative changes may exacerbate these problems.

4 Equity-REITs

Equity REITs own equities, i.e., real assets. A distinction must be made between mortgage REITs that only hold real estate securities and earn from their interest. Mortgage REITs have only book values or derivative values. Equity REITs earn income from rental income from investment properties. Metaphorically speaking, equity REITs invest in "bricks" and mortgage REITs in "paper".

In principle, equity REITs can cover all types of real estate related to a property or the buildings built on it. However, the tax exemption only applies to income from real estate. Many REITs offer their tenants services that go beyond the real estate purpose, e.g., the operation of a canteen in an office building. Here, such services are normally subject to trade tax.

REITs rarely manage a property themselves. Rather, this is done by the respective tenant, who is responsible for the operational business as the operator. REITs have nothing to do with business operations. Your profitability depends on the rental income and, thus, only indirectly on the business development of the operator.

The equities, i.e., the real assets in a REIT, can represent very different types of real estate. As a rule, individual REITs have a specific focus on one or a few industries. A clear separation of the focus of a REIT is not always possible, e.g., the transition from office buildings to commercial or retail buildings is often fluid. Therefore, you will find REITs in all categories that also conduct business from other categories.

In the following chapters, the individual focuses of REITs are broken down by industry. These chapters cover industries such as residentials, office buildings, retail (retail) to very specific industries such as prisons, casinos or agricultural properties.

4.1   Lodging

The hotel REITs industry - also called lodging - encompasses all types of real estate that deal with short-term rentals, mainly for overnight stays, vacation and tourism. Investments can include hotels and resorts, but also motels and holiday homes, as well as entire parks.

The hotel buildings are owned by the REIT. The actual operator of the hotel, e.g., a hotel brand like Hilton or Marriott, are tenants and pay the REIT an agreed rent. REITs often bought the buildings from the original brand and rented them back to them. This process is called sale-and-lease-back. It has the advantage for the seller that he slims down his balance sheet and gets liquid funds for growth again. The REIT gains a new investment and can usually generate income on long-term, predictable rental contracts.

Hotel or lodging REITs, however, have a peculiarity compared to other REITs: Often a rental payment is made to the REIT in the form of a pro rata share of the seasonal sales and depending on the number of guests and bookings. This makes them more sensitive to the economic downturn. If the hotel is booked less in times of crisis, the REIT also receives less rent. This is reinforced by the fact that in bad times, consumers make savings on their vacation trips and companies on business trips first.

Pebblebrooke Hotel Trust[1]

Pebblebrooke is a lodging REIT with a focus on hotels. The portfolio includes a large number of well-known hotel brands and resorts, e.g., Hilton, Hyatt, Marriott, Accor and many other smaller brands.

The REIT owns 42 hotels in 11 different cities, most of which are located on the east and West Coasts of the United States.

Pebblebrooke grew strongly through acquisitions of competitors, e.g., through the LaSalle Hotel Properties REIT.

In past economic crises, the REIT had to make substantial dividend cuts, which could be made up for in good times.

Name:	Pebblebrooke Hotel Trust
Ticker:	PEB
Sector:	Hotels

Market Capitalization:	1.98 billion USD
Dividend Yield:	6.38%
Payout-Ratio:	85.56%

Country of Origin:	USA
Core countries of investments:	USA

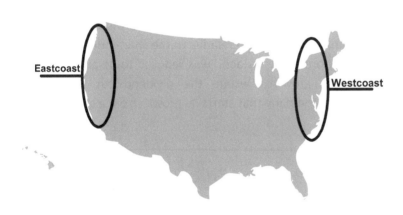

Leverage Ratio: 45%

Ashfort Hospitality Trust[2]

Ashfort Hospitality is a REIT focusing on high-end hotel properties with a full-service approach.

The focus is on the United States, but management reserves the right to invest outside of the United States, 119 hotel properties are owned, comprising a total of 25,000 rooms. The hotels are mainly operated by premium brands such as Marriott, Hilton, Ritz and Hyatt, with the first two representing the largest share of the portfolio.

A strong dividend cut was made in 2019. The price then fell so far that the original dividend yield relative to the share price was approximately restored. The dividend was reduced to be able to target liquidity to growth. Despite the dividend cut, new investors will find a company that starts its growth from a strong position.

Name:	Ashfort Hospitality Trust
Ticker:	AHT
Sector:	Hotels

Market Capitalization:	0,22 billion USD
Dividend Yield:	-
Payout-Ratio:	-

Country of Origin:	USA
Core countries of investments:	USA

Stability ✔
Diversification ✔
Yield ✔

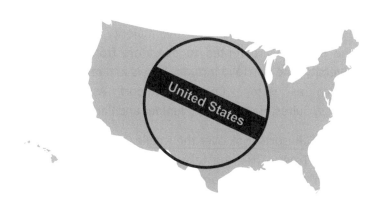

Leverage Ratio: 95%

Park Hotels & Resorts Inc.[3]

Park Hotels & Resorts is a spin-off from the Hilton Worldwide hotel chain. The Hilton hotel chain outsourced its properties to an independent company in 2017 and listed them as Park Hotels & Resorts Inc.

The portfolio includes urban hotels in city centers, resort hotels in popular holiday areas and airport hotels. The investments are in a prime location in cities such as Orlando, Los Angeles, San Francisco, Miami or New York. One focus is on hotels in Hawaii, which has been reduced from 25% to 20%. The portfolio also includes a Waldorf Astoria golf club.

Due to the past from the Hilton Group, the majority of the properties in the portfolio are rented to operators from the Hilton brand university. The portfolio includes hotels and resorts from brands such as Hilton, Conrad, Waldorf Astoria, DoubleTree, Embassy Suites, Hampton Inn, Juniper and Park 55.

In 2019, Park Hotels & Resorts took over the smaller competitor Chesapeake Lodging Trust. After the takeover, the REIT now owns 66 hotels with over 35,000 rooms, almost exclusively in the USA. With over $ 10 billion in investments, it has become the second-largest hotel REIT. Through the takeover, the portfolio was further expanded to include brands from the Marriott, Hyatt and IHG.

Name:	Park Hotels & Resorts Inc.
Ticker:	PK
Sector:	Hotels

Market Capitalization:	2.14 billion USD
Dividend Yield:	-
Payout-Ratio:	-

Country of Origin:	USA
Core countries of investments:	USA

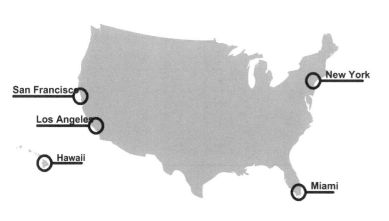

San Francisco

Los Angeles

Hawaii

New York

Miami

Leverage Ratio:

51%

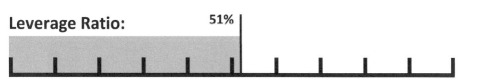

Sources

1 Pebblebrook Hotel Trust:
http://www.pebblebrookhotels.com/overview/
http://www.pebblebrookhotels.com/hotel-portfolio/
https://www.finanzen.net/aktien/pebblebrook_hotel_trust-aktie
https://seekingalpha.com/symbol/PEB

2 Ashfort Hospitality Trust:
https://www.ahtreit.com/overview
https://www.ahtreit.com/portfolio/investment-gallery
https://www.finanzen.net/aktien/ashford_hospitality_trust-aktie
https://seekingalpha.com/symbol/AHT?s=aht

3 Park Hotels & Resorts Inc.:
http://www.pkhotelsandresorts.com/
http://www.pkhotelsandresorts.com/portfolio
https://www.finanzen.net/aktien/park_hotelsresorts-aktie
https://seekingalpha.com/symbol/PK/dividends/scorecard?s=pk
http://www.pkhotelsandresorts.com/~/media/Files/P/Park-Hotels/reports-and-presentations/investor-deck-citi-2019.pdf

4.2   Residentials

Residentials are residential properties that are rented to private individuals and families for residential purposes. Residential REITs own apartments, flats and entire apartment blocks or residential areas. But you can also invest in student dormitories and in the US-made manufactured homes ("trailer parks"; cheap housing for caravans and mobile homes).

Opportunities and risks for residential REITs arise from the attractiveness of the location and its rent index, as well as from changes in the demographics and jobs in a region.

Regionally specialized REITs can benefit in rapidly growing markets, but can pay for them with falling rents and lost rent if such a region is disproportionately affected by relocation or unemployment.

Since private individuals are seen as particularly worthy of protection by the state, tenancy law or the possibility of rent increases is subject to strong regulation and political influence.

Essex Property Trust Inc.[4]

Essex Property owns a portfolio of 60,000 residential units worth over $ 17 billion. His properties are primarily on the West Coast of the United States, many in Silicon Valley. This region has one of the highest purchasing power and fastest growth rates in the United States. Especially in the big cities of California, there is a constant housing shortage, so the REIT can be sure of a good demand situation.

The REIT owns land with over 245 apartment buildings, the apartments of which are rented. The REIT attaches particular importance to the formation of communities in the respective neighborhoods.

Essex Property has consistently achieved a stable dividend with annual dividend increases over the years. The REIT can claim to have achieved the highest total return of all REITs since 1994.

Name:	Essex Property Trust Inc.
Ticker:	ESS
Sector:	Residential

Market Capitalization:	15.05 billion USD
Dividend Yield:	3.64%
Payout-Ratio:	62.60%

Country of Origin:	USA
Core countries of investments:	USA (Westcoast)

Stability ✓
Diversification ✓
Yield ✓

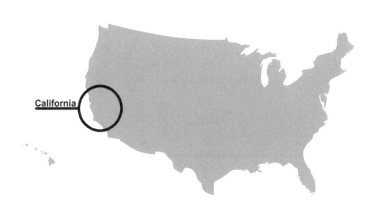

California

Leverage Ratio: 52%

Equity Lifestyle Properties Inc.[5]

Equity Lifestyle is a residential REIT in the United States. His properties appeal to tenants who value a high lifestyle. The REIT owns entire residential areas whose single-family houses are leased, senior housing, but also holiday homes, resorts and campsites with sophisticated equipment.

There are 411 properties in the portfolio. Often in popular holiday and residential areas, which offer upscale leisure activities such as playing golf and hiking.

The properties are spread across the United States and include over 145,000 apartments. Equity Lifestyle is the third-largest apartment owner in the United States.

Name:	Equity Lifestyle Properties Inc.
Ticker:	ELS
Sector:	Residential Senior Housing

Market Capitalization:	11.40 billion USD
Dividend Yield:	2.17%
Payout-Ratio:	65.91%

Country of Origin:	USA
Core countries of investments:	USA

Stability ✓
Diversification ✓
Yield ✓

Leverage Ratio: 69%

AvalonBay Communities Inc.[6]

AvalonBay is a REIT with an emphasis on apartments. The company owns over 78,000 residential units in metropolitan areas such as Washington, New York, Seattle and California.

The REIT has multi-family complexes that are rented to individual families and private individuals.

AvalonBay is the fourth-largest owner of apartments in the United States and has been in the market for over 20 years.

Name:	AvalonBay Communities Inc.
Ticker:	AVB
Sector:	Residential

Market Capitalization:	21.74 billion USD
Dividend Yield:	4.11%
Payout-Ratio:	69.53%

Country of Origin:	USA
Core countries of investments:	USA

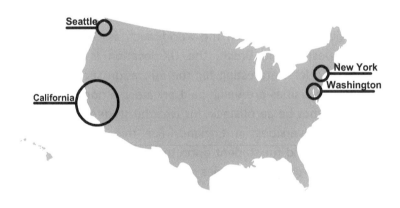

Seattle

New York

Washington

California

Leverage Ratio: 45%

Empiric Student Property Plc.[7]

Empiric Student Property is a British REIT with a focus on high-quality student dormitories. Besides the pure living space, the communities of the REIT also offer fitness studios, common rooms and cinemas. All dormitories are in a very good location and are within walking distance of universities, city centers or local public transport.

The REIT maintains 83 dormitories across the UK and is planning to develop 4 more dormitories.

Great Britain is still one of the most popular places to study with the most prestigious universities in the world, such as Oxford and Cambridge. Despite the Brexit, the UK location is not expected to become less interesting for the education sector. Since many elite universities are being paid privately, a non-EU membership should not be an obstacle for wealthy students to study at famous universities in England. For this reason, continued strong demand for student dormitories and stronger growth than in other property categories can be expected.

Name:	Empiric Student Property Plc.
Ticker:	EPCFF
Sector:	Student Housing

Market Capitalization:	0.44 billion USD
Dividend Yield:	1.49%
Payout-Ratio:	50%

Country of Origin:	UK
Core countries of investments:	UK

United Kingdom

Leverage Ratio: 37%

Equity-REITs

Office

Sources

4 Essex Property Trust:
https://www.essexapartmenthomes.com/about
https://www.finanzen.net/aktien/essex_property_trust-aktie
https://seekingalpha.com/symbol/ESS/dividends/scorecard?s=ess

5 Equity Lifestyle Properties Inc.:
https://www.equitylifestyleproperties.com/our-company
https://www.equitylifestyleproperties.com/our-portfolio
https://www.finanzen.net/aktien/equity_lifestyle_properties-aktie
https://seekingalpha.com/symbol/ELS/dividends/scorecard?s=els

6 AvalonBay Communities Inc.:
https://www.avaloncommunities.com/about-us
https://www.avaloncommunities.com/about-us/investor-relations
https://www.finanzen.net/aktien/avalonbay_communities-aktie
https://seekingalpha.com/symbol/AVB/dividends/scorecard?s=avb

7 Empiric Student Property Plc.:
https://www.empiric.co.uk/investment-portfolio
https://www.finanzen.net/aktien/empiric_student_property-aktie
https://seekingalpha.com/symbol/EPCFF

4.3 Office

Office REITs own office properties and high-rise buildings. The properties in the portfolio are rented as whole buildings, but also in parts as individual offices or on floors. Tenants are often companies, banks and public administrations.

Office properties are often outsourced to REITs as a sale-and-lease-back procedure. In this way, the outsourcing companies can optimize their balance sheet and liquidity. Many large companies only rent the majority of the properties they need instead of building them themselves. Even representative headquarters of large corporations are often rented. Office REITs can benefit from this practice and acquire high-quality real estate with solvent, long-term tenants.

Many office REITs focus on regional markets, such as US only, Europe only, or New York City only. An investor can thus selectively control the opportunities and risks of certain regions by choosing the REIT.

Since offices are easy to set up, there are often lower hurdles to market entry. Large REITs can counter this with existing properties in an excellent location.

However, office REITs are very cyclical. Rental contracts are often tied to inflation, and defaults, terminations or closings of large corporations occur more frequently in times of crisis.

Office

Empire State Realty Trust Inc.[8]

As the name suggests, the most significant investment of this REIT is the Empire State Building. The Empire State Building is one of the most famous buildings in the world and a world-famous landmark in New York. It includes offices, viewing platforms and retail space and is rented by large insurance companies, leasing agencies, advertising agencies, law firms and financial institutions. Although the focus is on office space, the Empire State Building's public viewing platforms alone generate $ 130 million a year in revenue. The Empire State Building is (and not only in New York) the No. 1 tourist attraction in the world and will probably remain so. It beats Disneyland, the Eiffel Tower and the Golden Gate Bridge in popularity. Even though there are many other skyscrapers with viewing platforms in New York, it is very difficult to copy the image and popularity of the Empire State Building.

It was privately owned until 2013 when the building complex, along with 29 other properties in New York and Connecticut, was listed on the stock exchange as REIT.

The portfolio includes office buildings and retail properties in the greater New York area, many in Manhattan and along the famous Broadway.

The largest shareholder is the Qatar Investment Authority (QIA), a sovereign wealth fund of the rich oil country Qatar

Name:	Empire State Realty Trust Inc.
Ticker:	ESRT
Sector:	Office

Market Capitalization:	1.16 billion USD
Dividend Yield:	6.38%
Payout-Ratio:	65.69%

Country of Origin:	USA
Core countries of investments:	USA (New York)

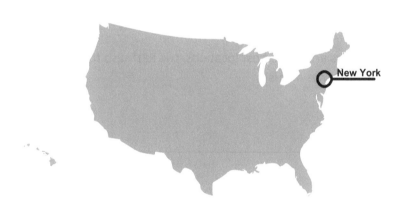

New York

Leverage Ratio: 60%

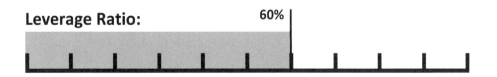

Office

Boston Properties Inc.[9]

Boston Properties was founded in 1970 and has upscale office buildings and business centers in its core markets of Boston, New York, San Francisco and Washington.

In San Francisco, the REIT has a 95% stake in the Salesforce Tower, which was built in 2018, the second tallest building on the West Coast of the USA.

The tenants of the buildings are the government of the USA, as well as many large companies, banks and technology companies.

A total of 48 million sf of office space is managed in 164 buildings.

As the investments are in the best locations, the REIT also found stable demand in times of crisis.

Name:	Boston Properties Inc.
Ticker:	BXP
Sector:	Office

Market Capitalization:	13.75 billion USD
Dividend Yield:	4.44%
Payout-Ratio:	54.87%

Country of Origin:	USA
Core countries of investments:	USA

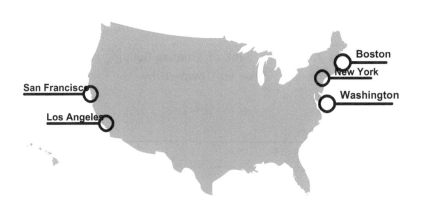

Leverage Ratio: 61%

Equity-REITs

Office

Vornado Realty Trust[10]

The Vornado Realty Trust is a REIT with a focus on office buildings and retail properties in New York, Chicago and San Francisco.

The REIT's properties are ideally located on Broadway and Times Square in Manhattan. The portfolio comprises 35 office buildings, 69 retail buildings, 1,991 apartments, a hotel and shares in other buildings or real estate companies.

Companies like Bloomberg and Amazon are tenants of Vornado office properties. The retail properties are in New York's most popular and expensive shopping areas such as Fifth Avenue, Madison Avenue, Times Square, Union Square and SoHo.

Vornado still owns 70% of the Bank of America Building in San Francisco. The remaining 30% are owned by the Trump Organization.

Name:	Vornado Realty Trust
Ticker:	VNO
Sector:	Office
	Retail

Market Capitalization:	7.75 billion USD
Dividend Yield:	7.37%
Payout-Ratio:	84.28%

Country of Origin:	USA
Core countries of investments:	USA

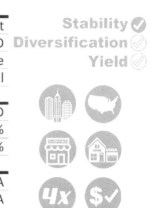

Stability ✓
Diversification ✓
Yield ✓

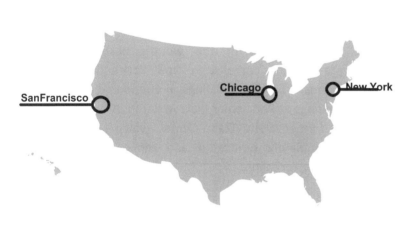

SanFrancisco

Chicago

New York

Leverage Ratio: 56%

Office

Brookfield Property REIT Inc.[11]

Brookfield Property REIT is a subsidiary of Brookfield Property Partners L.P. and simulates their dividend payment and dividend rhythm 1:1 in the form of a tax-privileged REIT. Brookfield Property Partners, in turn, is a real estate management subsidiary of Brookfield Asset Management Inc., one of the most influential private equity companies in the world, which manages investment for rich clients and institutional investors.

Brookfield Property has a diversified property portfolio across diverse industries. These include office, retail, industrial and residential properties and many more.

The portfolio includes some of the world's best-known properties, e.g., a building complex in New York's newest district, Hudson Yards, 11 office buildings in London's Canary Wharf and the buildings at Potsdamer Platz in Berlin. A building complex near the former World Trade Center, which was not destroyed, was completely renovated and reopened as a business center in New York City.

Brookfield also owns Center Parks and student residences in the UK.

Brookfield Property claims to be the largest property owner in many cities, including New York, Los Angeles and London.

Name:	Brookfield Property REIT Inc.
Ticker:	BPYU
Sector:	Diversified

Market Capitalization:	10.78 billion USD
Dividend Yield:	11.68%
Payout-Ratio:	23.76%

Country of Origin:	Canada
Core countries of investments:	USA
	Europe

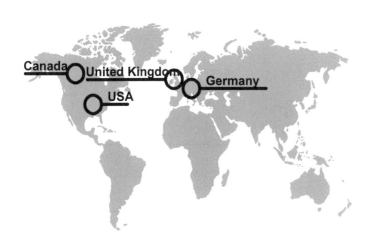

Leverage Ratio: 85%

Office

Hudson Pacific Properties Inc.[12]

Hudson Pacific Properties is a REIT focusing on real estate along the West Coast of the United States. In cities such as Los Angeles and San Francisco, 53 office buildings and 3 film studios are rented to large media companies and technology companies. They cover a total usable area of 20 million sf.

The Google parent Alphabet and Netflix are among the largest tenants of the REIT with over 10% of sales.

The largest shareholder is the Glaser Kochavi family, who are among the most influential real estate entrepreneurs in the United States.

Name:	Hudson Pacific Properties Inc.
Ticker:	HPP
Sector:	Film Studios Office

Market Capitalization:	3.7 billion USD
Dividend Yield:	4.21%
Payout-Ratio:	49.3%

Country of Origin:	USA
Core countries of investments:	USA (Westcoast)

Stability ✓
Diversification ✓
Yield ✓

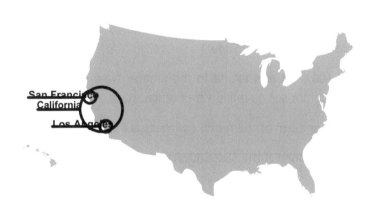

San Francisco
California
Los Angeles

Leverage Ratio: 52%

Office

SL Green Realty Corp.[13]

SL Green is the largest commercial rental company in New York. Of its 111 office properties, many are among the most famous buildings in New York. They are on Vanderbilt Avenue, Madison Avenue, Fifth Avenue, Avenue of the Americas, Broadway, SoHo, Columbus Circle and Times Square. The One Vanderbilt Building is currently under construction. When completed, it will be one of the most famous landmarks in Manhattan and will be rented out to the largest corporations in the financial world.

In addition, there are high-quality retail buildings and shopping centers in a prime New York location. The portfolio of SL Green includes the musical building in Times Square, which permanently houses the Lion King Show.

The REIT focuses 100% on real estate in the greater New York area. The portfolio comprises 48 million sf of office space.

The average remaining term of the rental contracts is 8.8 years.

The REIT share is a member of the S&P 500 share index.

Name:	SL Green Realty Corp.
Ticker:	SLG
Sector:	Office

Market Capitalization:	4.03 billion USD
Dividend Yield:	7.22%
Payout-Ratio:	51.40%

Country of Origin:	USA
Core countries of investments:	USA (New York)

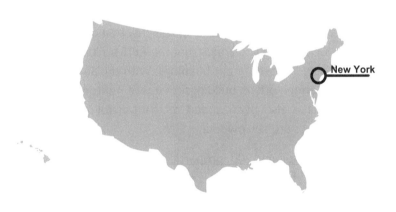

New York

Leverage Ratio: 55%

Office

Office Properties Income Trust[14]

Office Properties Trust started as a Government Properties Trust and focused exclusively on office properties for public buildings. The only tenants were government agencies, public corporations, state governments of the United States, and the United Nations. These authorities were seen as highly resilient tenants, who rarely terminate leases to change locations.

The REIT traditionally had a very low level of debt and could, therefore, be regarded as very crisis-proof and stable.

The REIT merged with the Select Income REIT to form today's Office Properties Income Trust. The naming and deletion of the part of the name "Government" clarifies that the REIT no longer only invests exclusively in government buildings. With the Select Income portfolio, normal office buildings that are rented to private companies have also been added to the portfolio. All previous public buildings are still owned.

The portfolio now comprises 200 properties, with extremely solvent and secure tenants also being used for non-governmental buildings. The original strategy continues unabated. 64% of tenants are investment-grade certified and 26% are still part of the US government.

Name:	Office Properties Income Trust
Ticker:	OPI
Sector:	Office
	Governmental Buildings
Market Capitalization:	1.2 billion USD
Dividend Yield:	8.94%
Payout-Ratio:	41.22%
Country of Origin:	USA
Core countries of investments:	USA

Stability ✓
Diversification ✓
Yield ✓

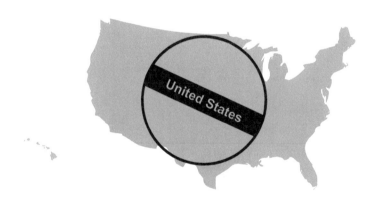

Leverage Ratio: 58%

Equity-REITs

Office

Dream Office Real Estate Investment Trust[15]

Dream Office Real Estate Investment Trust

The Dream Office REIT comes from Canada and is one of the largest office property owners in the country.

The portfolio only includes real estate in Canada, with a focus on the most populous city of Toronto. The largest tenants include the Government of Canada and several large Canadian and US banks.

Dream Office REIT continues to hold a 19.2% stake in Dream Industrial REIT, a REIT with a focus on industrial buildings in Canada and the United States.

Name:	Dream Office Real Estate Investment Trust
Ticker:	DRETF
Sector:	Office

Market Capitalization:	0.85 billion USD
Dividend Yield:	4.87%
Payout-Ratio:	33.63%

Country of Origin:	Canada
Core countries of investments:	Canada

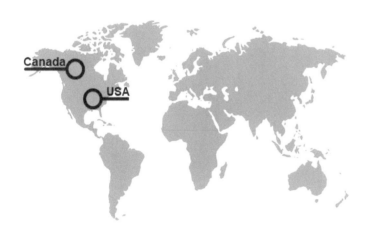

Leverage Ratio: 47%

Office

Alstria Office REIT AG[16]

Alstria Office REIT is a German company based in Hamburg. It is one of the few REITs registered in Germany and focuses on the ownership and management of office and commercial property in Germany.

The investments are in Dusseldorf, Frankfurt, Hamburg, Hanover, Munich and Stuttgart.

The portfolio comprises 116 buildings with a usable area of 16 million sf with a value of USD 4.74 billion. The most important tenants are the city of Hamburg, Daimler and Deutsche Telekom.

Name:	Alstria Office REIT AG
Ticker:	ALSRF
Sector:	Office

Market Capitalization:	2.66 billion USD
Dividend Yield:	3.87%
Payout-Ratio:	16.2%

Country of Origin:	Germany
Core countries of investments:	Germany

Leverage Ratio: 37%

Office

Embassy Office Parks REIT[17]

Embassy Office Parks is a REIT from India and was the only REIT from this country to go public in April 2019. A second Indian REIT has already planned to go public in 2020. Then a Blackstone joint venture is to be listed on the stock exchange. If the development succeeds, further IPOs of real estate can be expected, because despite the size of India, domestic companies still find it difficult to attract foreign capital.

Embassy plans and develops office buildings and business parks in major cities in India. A business park is an entire campus of office and research buildings on a single piece of land. Different companies rent them and can benefit from the proximity to each other and the shared infrastructure. Most of the business parks have respective focus areas, such as IT, technology, bio-tech, life science parks, etc.

Embassy is India's largest private owner of office real estate. The portfolio includes real estate with 32 million sf of usable space, a further 13 million sf are being planned. The business parks are in major Indian cities such as Bangalore and Mumbai, which are very much shaped by the service and IT sectors. Embassy's customers include technology groups such as Google or Microsoft.

The REIT continues to operate a 460-hectare solar park to be able to supply its buildings with sustainably produced energy.

Name:	Embassy Office Parks REIT	
Ticker:	EMBASSY	
Sector:	Office	

Market Capitalization:	-
Dividend Yield:	7.11%
Payout-Ratio:	-

Country of Origin:	India
Core countries of investments:	India

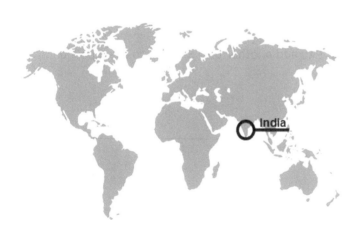

Leverage Ratio 30%

Office

Land Securities Group Plc.[18]

The Land Securities Group, also called Landsec, is an office REIT from Great Britain. It is one of the largest real estate companies in Europe and the largest REIT in the UK. He owns 106 properties across the UK. 65% of the properties are located directly in London.

The majority of the portfolio includes office buildings, but also some residential and retail properties. The entire property portfolio has a usable area of 26 million sf.

The REIT also owns the "Piccadilly Lights" building on Piccadilly Circus in London, where the world-famous billboards are attached.

Landsec has plans to add another USD 3 billion to the pipeline in the coming years.

Name:	Land Securities Group Plc.
Ticker:	LSGOF
Sector:	Office
	Retail

Market Capitalization:	5.44 billion USD
Dividend Yield:	3.76%
Payout-Ratio:	41%

Country of Origin:	UK
Core countries of investments:	UK

United Kingdom

Leverage Ratio: 39%

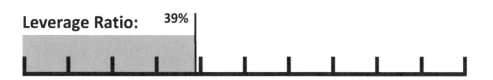

Equity-REITs

Office

Sources

8 Empire State Realty Trust Inc.
https://www.empirestaterealtytrust.com/about-us/
https://www.empirestaterealtytrust.com/properties/
https://youtu.be/qlxLXQUvOa8
https://www.finanzen.net/aktien/empire_state_realty_trust_a-aktie
https://seekingalpha.com/symbol/ESRT

9 Boston Properties Inc.:
http://www.bostonproperties.com/pages/about
http://www.bostonproperties.com/pages/properties
https://www.finanzen.net/aktien/boston_properties-aktie
https://seekingalpha.com/symbol/BXP/dividends/scorecard?s=bxp

10 Vornado Realty Trust:
https://www.vno.com/about/overview
https://www.vno.com/portfolio/overview
https://www.finanzen.net/aktien/vornado_realty_trust-aktie
https://seekingalpha.com/symbol/VNO/dividends/scorecard?s=vno

11 Brookfield Property REIT Inc.:
https://www.brookfield.com/our-businesses/real-estate
https://www.finanzen.net/aktien/brookfield_property_reit-aktie
https://seekingalpha.com/symbol/BPR/dividends/scorecard?s=bpr

12 Hudson Pacific Properties Inc.:
https://s22.q4cdn.com/675150095/files/doc_presentations/2019/9/09-20/Q2-2019-HPP-Investor-Deck-090419-FINAL-(2).pdf
https://www.hudsonpacificproperties.com/about
https://www.finanzen.net/aktien/hudson_pacific_properties-aktie
https://seekingalpha.com/symbol/HPP/dividends/scorecard?s=hpp

13 SL Green Realty Corp.:
https://slgreen.com/about
https://slgreen.com/properties
https://www.finanzen.net/aktien/sl_green_realty-aktie
https://seekingalpha.com/symbol/SLG/dividends/scorecard?s=slg
https://slgreen.gcs-web.com/static-files/8e49a27c-5167-43f8-97e3-656c06eef5fb

14 Office Properties Income Trust:
https://www.opireit.com/home/default.aspx
https://www.opireit.com/properties/default.aspx
https://www.finanzen.net/aktien/office_properties-aktie
https://seekingalpha.com/symbol/OPI/dividends/scorecard?s=opi

15 Dream Office Real Estate Investment Trust:
https://www.dream.ca/office/about-us/
https://www.dream.ca/office/portfolio/
https://www.finanzen.net/aktien/dream_global_real_estate_investment_trust_units-aktie
https://seekingalpha.com/symbol/DRETF

16 Alstria Office REIT AG:
https://alstria.de/
https://alstria.de/portfolio/#mapSection
https://www.finanzen.net/aktien/alstria_office_reit-aktie
https://seekingalpha.com/symbol/ALSRF/dividends/no_dividends_history?s=alsrf

17 Embassy Office Park REIT:
https://www.embassyofficeparks.com/about/
http://ir.embassyofficeparks.com/investors/investor-overview/default.aspx
https://www.finanzen.net/aktien/embassy_office_parks_reit_registered-aktie

18 Land Securities Group Plc.:
https://landsec.com/properties
https://landsec.com/sites/default/files/2019-09/Landsec%20Capital%20Markets%20Day%202019%20-%20presentation%20slides.pdf
https://www.finanzen.net/aktien/land_securities-aktie
https://seekingalpha.com/symbol/LSGOF

4.4 Healthcare

Healthcare REITs encompass all properties that focus on healthcare. These include hospitals, health centers, medical centers, nursing homes and retirement homes.

Medical buildings have special requirements e.g., to ensure cleanliness and sterility, supply of oxygen to the rooms, furnishing the rooms, waste disposal, operating theaters, emergency buttons, division of the rooms (treatment rooms, operating theaters, waiting rooms, reception) as well as security and access restrictions to certain departments , For this reason, the construction of a healthcare building requires special expertise. Normal buildings cannot easily be converted into a healthcare building.

The healthcare and health care sector is relatively independent of the economic cycle. The demographic change also leads to a longer life expectancy and a higher proportion of the older population in the industrialized countries. In the United States alone, the share of the over 65 population will soon grow to over 35%, as it is precisely the generation of baby boomers reaching this age. Health care services and senior housing are benefiting from this trend and increasing demand.

REITs usually own the buildings and rent them to the actual operators, e.g., Hospital and nursing home operators. They rent the buildings with long-term leases, often supported by public bodies.

Opportunities arise from specialized facilities necessary to supply the population and cannot simply change location. Healthcare is a stable industry even in times of crisis, as illness and age are independent of the economy. But the industry is subject to an increased political risk, which in the USA e.g., revealed by the ailing or partially non-existent health insurance system.

Healthcare REITs can rent their properties to state operators or to private ones. State operators are safer because the health infrastructure is often politically dominated or permanently desired. Private operators, on the other hand, promise higher profit margins but also a higher risk of giving up a location if there is no profitability. In times of crisis, there is a risk that parts of the population can no longer afford private health services.

The location depends on whether certain locations in urban areas are subject to strong regional competition or whether e.g., there is almost a monopoly in rural areas.

Healthpeak Properties Inc.[19]

Healthpeak is a REIT in the healthcare industry. Its portfolio includes hospitals, medical buildings and science campuses in San Francisco, Boston and San Diego, medical office buildings near large hospitals and 27,000 units for nursing homes and assisted living.

Furthermore, tenants are offered various real estate services via subsidiaries, e.g., Maintenance, green space work and security services. As with many other REITs, these non-real estate-related services are exempt from tax exemptions for REITs - pure rents remain tax-free at company level.

The entire portfolio includes $ 20 billion in real estate.

The REIT has steadily increased its dividend since it was founded and has not had to make any cuts even in the 2008/09 financial crisis.

Name:	Healthpeak Properties Inc.
Ticker:	PEAK
Sector:	Hospitals Medical Buildings Science Campuses
Market Capitalization:	14.76 billion USD
Dividend Yield:	5.47%
Payout-Ratio:	90.60%
Country of Origin:	USA
Core countries of investments:	USA

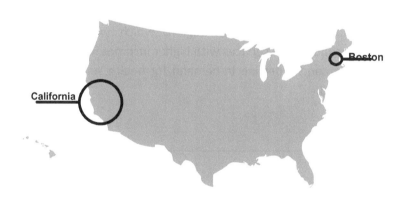

California

Boston

Leverage Ratio: 51%

First Real Estate Investment Trust[20]

First Real Estate is Singapore's first investment trust for real estate in healthcare. The investment strategy encompasses a broad portfolio of real estate in the healthcare and healthcare sector in Asia.

The portfolio includes a high quality and diversified portfolio of 20 properties, including 16 in Indonesia, three in Singapore and one in South Korea with a combined value of over $ 1.3 billion. The portfolio consists of hospitals, nursing homes, rehabilitation centers and other healthcare facilities.

The location focus in Southeast Asia benefits from the growing middle and upper classes in this region, which will also increasingly demand health services with higher incomes. Both a decline in income and a decline in demand for health services cannot be assumed.

Name:	First Real Estate Investment Trust
Ticker:	FESNF
Sector:	Hospitals

Market Capitalization:	0.41 billion USD
Dividend Yield:	5.88%
Payout-Ratio:	75%

Country of Origin:	Singapore
Core countries of	Singapore
investments:	Indonesia
	South Korea

Stability
Diversification ✓
Yield ✓

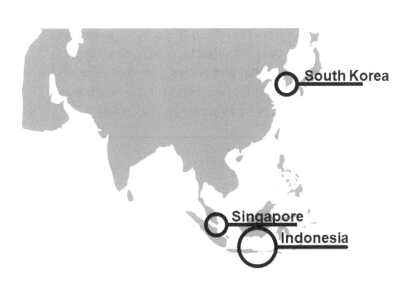

Leverage Ratio: ??%

LTC Properties Inc.[21]

LTC is a REIT for retirement homes. He owns 204 properties in 28 U.S. states that have been rented by 30 operators.

The portfolio consists of 50% pure residential units with a target group geared towards seniors. The other half consists of dormitories that offer an expanded medical care program and provide the relevant specialist staff. Both medical services and staff are managed by the tenants. The REIT only acts as a landlord.

The portfolio continues to be diversified, with a mix of privately paid services and those paid by the government.

LTC has acquired many properties from the original operators through sale-and-lease-back contracts but also grants mortgages, subordinated capital and enters into joint ventures with partner companies. It, therefore, represents a mixture of residential and healthcare as well as equity and mortgage REIT.

Name:	LTC Properties Inc.
Ticker:	LTC
Sector:	Senior Housing

Market Capitalization:	1.47 billion USD
Dividend Yield:	6.1%
Payout-Ratio:	77.82%

Country of Origin:	USA
Core countries of investments:	USA

Leverage Ratio: 47%

Ventas Inc.[22]

Ventas is a REIT from the healthcare industry. He owns 360 medical office buildings, which make up 35% of the portfolio. They include offices near the clinic or university, research buildings and real estate that house medical practices or medical centers.

6% of the portfolio includes hospitals and specialist clinics, such as Cancer centers.

The majority of the investments, however, consist of retirement homes, of which 33% of the portfolio are operated and another 21% are leased using the NNN procedure.

All lines of business together comprise 1,200 buildings. These are in 40 states in the USA as well as in Great Britain and Canada. In total, they are rented to 29 operators.

Almost all services offered in the Ventas facilities are paid for privately by the patient. The REIT's income is, therefore, less dependent on risks from US public health policies.

Name:	Ventas Inc.
Ticker:	VTR
Sector:	Senior Housing
	Medical Buildings
	Hospitals
Market Capitalization:	13.32 billion USD
Dividend Yield:	7.98%
Payout-Ratio:	89.03%
Country of Origin:	USA
Core countries of investments:	USA

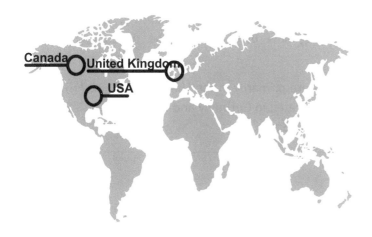

Leverage Ratio: 59%

Medical Properties Trust Inc.[23]

In contrast to many other healthcare REITs, the Medical Properties Trust only has correct and full-fledged hospitals, including emergency surgery, rehabilitation, long-term and special clinics.

The portfolio has grown in recent years through asset acquisitions of $ 6 billion, making the Medical Properties Trust the second largest non-governmental hospital owner in the United States.

The REIT not only acts as a pure landlord but also offers various financial assistance for its customers, e.g., financing, sale-and-lease-back, developing new buildings and the expansion of existing hospitals.

The portfolio's clinics are primarily in the United States (82.7%). In Europe, 14.8% are located in Germany and a small part (2.8%) in Italy, Great Britain and Spain.

Name:	Medical Properties Trust Inc.
Ticker:	MPW
Sector:	Hospitals
Market Capitalization:	9.73 billion USD
Dividend Yield:	5.86%
Payout-Ratio:	69.12%
Country of Origin:	USA
Core countries of investments:	USA Europe

Stability ✓
Diversification ✓
Yield ✓

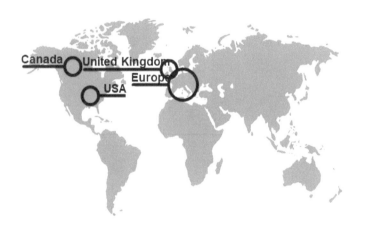

Canada United Kingdom Europe USA

Leverage Ratio: 54%

Omega Healthcare Investors Inc.[24]

Omega Healthcare is a health REIT for nursing homes and medically assisted living. The REIT owns 910 buildings in the USA and Great Britain, which it rents to around 70 operating companies. The tenants are broadly diversified, so only one operator accounts for over 10% of total sales.

The services offered in the facilities are both paid for by the Medicare and Medicaid state health insurance programs and paid for privately. The REIT, therefore, sees itself more robustly armed against falling demand e.g., because of political changes in the health system.

The properties in the portfolio are provided using the triple net procedure with fixed rents and contractually agreed rent increases

Name:	Omega Healthcare Investors Inc.
Ticker:	OHI
Sector:	Senior Housing

Market Capitalization:	6.81 billion USD
Dividend Yield:	9.17%
Payout-Ratio:	89.16%

Country of Origin:	USA
Core countries of investments:	USA UK

Stability ✓
Diversification ✓
Yield ✓

Leverage Ratio: 58%

Welltower Inc.[25]

Welltower is a REIT specializing in U.S. nursing homes, assisted living, senior residences and medical office buildings. He owns 1,502 health care properties. Tenants of the real estate are the largest chains for senior care facilities in the United States.

Some hospitals and other healthcare buildings are held outside the United States.

A special feature is that over 93% of its facilities are paid for privately by its customers and patients. This strategy makes the REIT independent of political risks, e.g., the cancellation of health care for the population.

Name:	Welltower Inc.
Ticker:	WELL
Sector:	Senior Housing

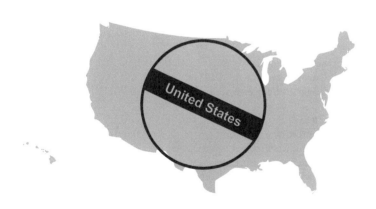

Market Capitalization:	20.85 billion USD
Dividend Yield:	4.88%
Payout-Ratio:	70.24%

Country of Origin:	USA
Core countries of investments:	USA

Stability ✓
Diversification ✓
Yield ✓

Leverage Ratio: 47%

Sources

19 Healthpeak Properties Inc.:
https://www.healthpeak.com/about-us/
https://www.healthpeak.com/properties/
https://www.finanzen.net/aktien/hcp-aktie
https://seekingalpha.com/symbol/PEAK?s=peak

20 First Real Estate Investment Trust:
https://www.finanzen.net/aktien/first_real_estate_investment_trust-aktie
https://www.first-reit.com/portfolio-overview.html
https://seekingalpha.com/symbol/FESNF

21 LTC Properties Inc.:
https://www.ltcreit.com/about/
https://www.ltcreit.com/portfolio/
https://www.finanzen.net/aktien/ltc_properties-aktie
https://seekingalpha.com/symbol/LTC

22 Ventas Inc.:
https://www.ventasreit.com/
https://www.ventasreit.com/our-portfolio
https://www.finanzen.net/aktien/ventas-aktie
https://seekingalpha.com/symbol/VTR/dividends/scorecard?s=vtr

23 Medical Properties Trust Inc.:
http://www.medicalpropertiestrust.com/
http://www.medicalpropertiestrust.com/content.asp?id=314964
https://www.finanzen.net/aktien/medical_properties_trust-aktie
https://seekingalpha.com/symbol/MPW/dividends/scorecard?s=mpw

24 Omega Healthcare Investors Inc.:
http://www.omegahealthcare.com/
http://www.omegahealthcare.com/portfolio/map-of-our-locations
https://www.finanzen.net/aktien/omega_healthcare_investors-aktie
https://seekingalpha.com/symbol/OHI/dividends/scorecard?s=ohi
http://www.omegahealthcare.com/how-we-work/investor-thesis
http://www.omegahealthcare.com/~/media/Files/O/Omega-
HealthCare/2019/November%202019%20Investor%20Presentation.pdf

25 Welltower Inc.
https://welltower.com/about-us/
https://www.finanzen.net/aktien/welltower_1-aktie
https://seekingalpha.com/symbol/WELL/dividends/scorecard?s=well

4.5   Retail

Retail REITs include all types of buildings that provide retail space for retail. As a rule, the tenants are sellers to individual or end customers, i.e., private individuals or households. The most common branches of the tenants are fashion, food, accessories shops or gastronomy.

A sub-category of retail REITs are operators of large malls in which a large number of small shops are rented to individual shops and restaurants. Malls offer all kinds of trade, gastronomy and entertainment under one roof. This concept originated in the United States and has spread to high-income countries or regions in recent decades. With the advent of internet trading, a decline in customers has been noticed in many regions.

In contrast to malls, there are also retail buildings that consist of detached properties. These are often within easy reach of transport hubs and metropolitan areas. They can include shopping centers, supermarkets, hardware stores, fitness studios, cinemas, car dealerships, free-standing restaurants as well as kiosks and petrol stations.

Retail REITs can also invest in individual buildings in busy shopping arcades without managing the entire shopping area. You often own large buildings, on the ground floors of which the shop windows are located. Offices or apartments are often rented on the upper floors, so the transition to the "Residential" or "Office" category is often fluid.

The opportunities and risks of a retail REIT result from the consumer behavior of the end customers who shop in the shops of the tenants. Risks arise from changes in

social trends, such as online shopping or delivery services that bring purchases straight to your home. In such scenarios, sales for floor trading can decrease, making the tenants of the REITs less solvent or negotiating lower rents.

Trade depends also on fluctuations in the economy and the income situation of the population. Crises can severely damage the demand for more expensive or exclusive products (e.g., fashion, luxury items, cars), while businesses that deal with cheaper items or everyday items can benefit or at least remain unaffected by crises.

Opportunities arise from the location of the property and the effects of megatrends. For example, well-positioned properties in the world's top cities (New York, London, Paris) or in regions gaining popularity and purchasing power (Hong Kong, Singapore) can continue to show demand and rising rents even in crises. But also regionally successful locations, e.g., where little competition or no alternatives exist, can be successfully operated.

As with all REITs, the success of retail REITs lies in management and diversification. To protect yourself from unfavorable developments, a low-risk REIT should be broad and include both a higher number of different individual tenants, as well as industries, regions and target groups.

Realty Income Corp.[26]

Realty Income is one of the oldest and best-known REITs, it has existed for over 50 years and has been listed on the stock exchange for over 25 years. The REIT can have a very steady history of dividend increases - the dividend has never been cut. Due to its monthly payment, the REIT has secured the trademark rights to the slogan "The Monthly Dividend Company". Since 1994, the REIT has had an average total return of 16.8% a year. According to the official definition, Realty Income is one of the few REITs among the aristocratic dividends.

There are 5,900 buildings in the portfolio that are rented to 274 tenants in 49 US states. The investments are mainly free-standing retail buildings. His tenants include 7-Eleven shops, AMC cinemas, Wal-Mart supermarkets, Walgreens pharmacies and fitness studios. Industrial buildings (120 units) are also held to a lesser extent, e.g., Logistics building for Coca-Cola, but also 42 office buildings and 15 agricultural areas. The top tenants continue to include FedEx, Sainsburys, CVS Pharmacy, Kroger and Home Depot. There are also petrol station shops, Starbucks branches and fast food restaurants for chains such as Chipotle or Chick-A-Filet. The REIT's investments are limited to the USA and Great Britain

With a new program, Realty Income is adding additional income to its buildings by installing ATMs and solar panels, renting billboards, offering electric car charging stations and allowing cell phone towers on its buildings.

Name:	Realty Income Corp.
Ticker:	O
Sector:	Retail

Market Capitalization:	20.14 billion USD
Dividend Yield:	4.78%
Payout-Ratio:	85.48%

Country of Origin	USA
Core countries of	USA
investments:	UK

United Kingdom

USA

Leverage Ratio: 45%

Simon Property Group Inc.[27]

Simon Property is a retail REIT with a focus on malls, shopping centers and outlet centers. It is the largest retail REIT in the United States in this category. Simon Property is also the largest REIT listed in the S&P 500 stock market index.

Its portfolio includes 230 buildings with 190 million sf of retail space. Tenants are mainly retail shops and restaurants in the malls, e.g., Polo Ralph Lauren or Nike. The portfolio also includes a small number of hotels (9 pieces) and office buildings (10 pieces).

The centers are also in particularly lucrative locations with wealthy customers in the catchment area. There is also a shopping center in the Caesars Palace Casino in Las Vegas.

To encourage buyers to linger as long as possible, the malls from Simon Property are also rented to a variety of entertainment facilities. Many centers include cinemas, playgrounds or indoor adventure parks.

Besides the core market in the USA, the REIT's investments are widely spread around the world to achieve a high degree of diversification. He owns buildings in metropolitan areas in Germany, Japan, South Korea, Italy, Great Britain, Malaysia, Mexico, Canada and Thailand.

Simon Property also owns a venture fund that invests in startups that focus on connecting technology and retail. Simon contributes to the industry with capital and his network and can thus integrate the latest technologies in his centers at an early stage.

Name:	Simon Property Group Inc.
Ticker:	SPG
Sector:	Retail
	Shopping Malls
Market Capitalization:	23.23 billion USD
Dividend Yield:	11.53%
Payout-Ratio:	73.89%
Country of Origin:	USA
Core countries of investments:	USA
	Global

Stability
Diversification ✓
Yield ✓

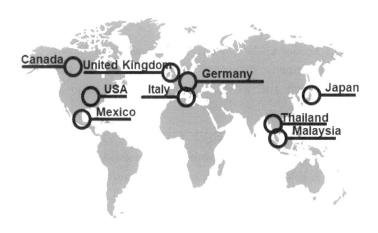

Leverage Ratio: 92%

National Retail Properties Inc.[28]

National retail is a REIT that belongs to freestanding average buildings. To see such as the gyms, cinemas, freestanding restaurants and steakhouses, bowling alleys, gas stations, car washes, 7-eleven stores and others.

Differentiate themselves 3,047 properties owned, which represent a usable area of almost 32 million sf. All properties have been taken care of in the USA and can be found in the fast all people.

The REIT has a history of 30 years of conservative planning and steady dividend increases. This gives him the status of a dividend certification right.

The major rating agencies have left the REIT with investment grade status. This means a quality characteristic and the creditworthiness, which also exists institutional supervision in the company.

National retailers have sold the stock ticker and advertising slogan "Die NNN-Gesellschaft", an abbreviation of the triple net procedure, which is relevant for the rental agreements for the properties.

Name:	National Retail Properties Inc.
Ticker:	NNN
Sector:	Retail
Market Capitalization:	5.93 billion USD
Dividend Yield:	5.97%
Payout-Ratio:	77.62%
Country of Origin:	USA
Core countries of investments:	USA

Stability ✓
Diversification ✓
Yield ✓

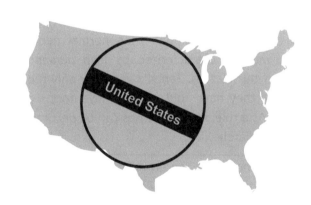

Leverage Ratio: 44%

Tanger Factory Outlets[29]

Tanger Factory Outlet operates outlet centers from major brands that could not be sold last season.

The REIT does not have locations in the form of large malls, but independent centers. The category of outlet centers shows a differentiated rhythm depending on the economic situation than regular retail REITs. In a crisis, the merchandise shifts more towards cheaper fashion and away from the latest collections. Tanger Factory Outlets is, therefore, suitable as an admixture to a risk-averse portfolio.

The REIT has 44 centers in the USA and, due to its targeted target group, has less competition than normal department stores. The business is characterized by high demand from tenants and short-term leases. Tenants generally only rent for a short period until they have sold off their inventory from the previous season. As a rule, expiring leases can be decorated and re-let almost immediately.

The REIT has been increasing the dividend regularly for over 25 years and is, therefore, one of the dividend aristocrats.

Name:	Tanger Factory Outlets
Ticker:	SKT
Sector:	Outlet Centers

Market Capitalization:	0.67 billion USD
Dividend Yield:	-
Payout-Ratio:	-

Country of Origin:	USA
Core countries of investments:	USA

Stability ✓
Diversification ✓
Yield ✓

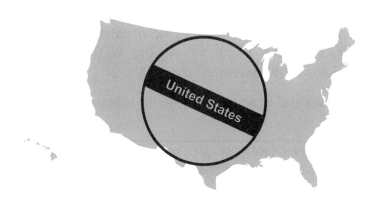

Leverage Ratio: 87%

Gazit Globe Ltd.[30]

Gazit Globe is a REIT from Israel that invests in 20 countries around the world. The REIT's portfolio includes supermarkets and shopping centers as well as healthcare buildings.

With 592 buildings and 6.7 million sf of usable space, it is one of the larger listed REITs despite its country of origin, which is rather unknown to REITs. Unfortunately, the REIT is only listed on the Tel Aviv and Nasdaq stock exchanges.

Gazit Globe has a 45.3% stake in Equity One, a REIT that specializes in supermarkets, pharmacies and retail spaces in the United States.

A subsidiary company ProMed Properties Inc. rents offices and research centers for the healthcare industry in the area surrounding hospitals and universities in the USA.

The Canadian business is again held through the subsidiary First Capital.

A European subsidiary, Citycon Oyj. owns and develops shopping centers and commercial space in Denmark, Sweden, Norway and Estonia. Additional buildings are in Bulgaria, Macedonia, Israel and Brazil. This makes Gazit Globe one of the most diversified REITs in the retail category worldwide.

Name:	Gazit Globe Ltd.
Ticker:	GZTGF
Sector:	Retail
	Shopping Malls

Market Capitalization:	0.93 billion USD
Dividend Yield:	8.64%
Payout-Ratio:	73.53%

Country of Origin:	Israel
Core countries of	Israel
investments:	USA
	Europe

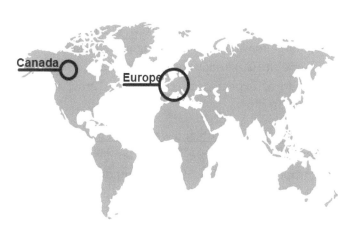

Leverage Ratio: 62%

Link Real Estate Investment Trust[31]

Link is a REIT from Hong Kong. It is the first REIT from this country and the largest in Asia. Its portfolio consists of retail space (76%), parking garages with 56,000 spaces (16%) and office buildings (8.3%) in Hong Kong and on the Chinese mainland in the cities of Beijing, Shanghai, Guangzhou and Shenzhen.

In Hong Kong, the REIT has 126 buildings with 7,999 million sf usable area and in China there are 5 buildings with 5 million sf area.

Its large retail buildings include large malls, shopping centers, megastores, supermarkets and shopping plazas. In Asia, the form of shopping for large malls is far from being as widespread as in the USA, where it is already on the decline. Asian consumers are, therefore, expected to continue to grow in retail.

Link sees himself still on a growth path and wants to achieve this through further acquisitions. The core market remains Hong Kong and Tier 1 metropolises in China. However, other regional markets are not excluded.

Name:	Link Real Estate
	Investment Trust
Ticker:	-
Sector:	Retail
	Shopping Malls
Market Capitalization:	17.24 billion USD
Dividend Yield:	4.38%
Payout-Ratio:	101.38%
Country of Origin:	Hongkong
Core countries of	Hongkong
investments:	China

Stability ✓
Diversification ✓
Yield ✓

22%

Leverage Ratio:

Fortune REIT[32]

Fortune REIT is one of the first REITs to be founded in Hong Kong. It has 16 shopping malls with a total area of 3 million sf and 2713 parking spaces.

All investments are in Hong Kong. There are no buildings on mainland China. The REIT shares are listed on the Hong Kong and Singapore stock exchanges.

The Hong Kong location is a dynamic and profitable location with high economic growth and a direct connection to China's technology region Shenzhen. However, Hong Kong has the peculiarity that the country has been leased by the government of China for 99 years. This lease expires in 2047. After that time, it depends on the Chinese government how it intends to deal politically with property owners and on what terms it will extend any contracts. This creates a long-term risk for all REIT investments in Hong Kong, as China's future policies are difficult to predict and are still shaped by communist rather than economic ideals.

Name:	Fortune REIT
Ticker:	-
Sector:	Retail
	Shopping Malls

Market Capitalization:	1.95 billion USD
Dividend Yield:	6.36%
Payout-Ratio:	111.36%

Country of Origin:	Hongkong
Core countries of investments:	Hongkong

Stability
Diversification
Yield

Hongkong

24%

Leverage Ratio:

Scentre Group[33]

The Scentre Group is a REIT from Australia in the category Retail REITs. The REIT owns shopping centers and retail properties in Australia and New Zealand. There are 41 shopping centers with 12,544 individual shops in its portfolio.

Scentre is a spin-off from the former Westfield Group and operates shopping centers under the Westfield brand. The Westfield Group split in 2014, creating a REIT for all Australian real estate with Scentre, while the European and American market merged with a European competitor to Unibail-Rodamco-Westfield.

The Scentre Group owns the buildings of the shopping centers and takes on tasks such as development, design, construction, asset management, property management, leasing and marketing for them. His investments are in major Australian cities such as Sydney, Canberra, Brisbane, Auckland and Melbourne.

The Scentre Group is very well suited for the regional diversification of a REIT depot, since the Australian economy runs in different cycles than the economy in Europe and North America. Due to a strongly raw material economy and the regional proximity to Asia, these factors influence the Australian economy more than the American domestic demand or the European government debt to other retail REITs would. This also affects the Australian dollar, in which the stock is quoted, which can reduce a cluster risk from excessive investments in USD.

Name:	Scentre Group
Ticker:	STGPF
Sector:	Retail
	Shopping Malls

Market Capitalization:	7.61 billion USD
Dividend Yield:	4.66%
Payout-Ratio:	52.63%

Country of Origin:	Australia
Core countries of	Australia
investments:	New Zealand

Stability Diversification Yield

Leverage Ratio: 41%

Hamborner REIT AG[34]

The Hamborner REIT is a REIT for retail properties and office buildings. In major cities, his investments are only made in Germany.

The portfolio includes larger office buildings and retail properties, such as large-scale retail properties, supermarkets, specialty market centers, hypermarkets, hardware stores and commercial buildings in central city center locations. The tenants of the properties are well-known local chains such as Obi, Saturn, Kaufland, Edeka or Real.

In total, the REIT owns 79 properties, of which 62% of sales come from retail and 34% from office buildings. The regional focus is on strong growth regions in the south as well as in the west and southwest of Germany.

The historical roots of the REIT come from the wealth management of the industrial family of the Thyssens, who separated their real estate holdings from the coal mining and steel processing industries.

The RAG Foundation still holds 12.45% of the shares. It is a state-owned foundation to finance the exit of German coal mining. Grade foundations have a long-term investment horizon and depend on reliable, stable and regular income. Because of this, an investor can expect the RAG-Stiftung as anchor shareholder to have a long-term positive influence on business policy and to steer it to the advantage of the other shareholders.

Name:	Hamborner REIT AG
Ticker:	-
Sector:	Retail

Market Capitalization:	0.78 billion USD
Dividend Yield:	5.13%
Payout-Ratio:	250%

Country of Origin:	Germany
Core countries of investments:	Germany

Leverage Ratio: 58%

Deutsche Konsum REIT AG[35]

Deutsche Konsum is a REIT for retail properties in established shopping locations away from major cities. The core market is regional locations, to a large extent in the new federal states of eastern Germany.

The company fills the niche of investments too big for private investors but too small for institutional investors. Since there are few professional players in this supposedly unattractive sector, the REIT promises opportunities through acquisitions and professional management to revitalize undervalued properties at a profit. Due to its size, it uses the advantage of having a better negotiating position with tenants than previous owners, who are mostly individuals with a small number of properties. Its portfolio includes hardware stores, specialty stores and supermarkets. In total, there are 123 properties with a sales area of 8 million sf. The main tenants are supermarkets such as Edeka, Aldi, Rewe, Norma or Lidl (approx. 50% of the portfolio). The rest includes hardware stores as well as clothing stores such as Deichmann, Takko or Kik and other industries.

By concentrating on tenants who cover the daily needs of the population, the REIT hopes to generate a stable income stream that will remain unaffected by economic cycles.

The REIT is mainly positioned in markets that, due to their rather secondary position, are not at risk of online food retail, as large e-commerce providers concentrate on larger metropolitan areas.

Name:	Deutsche Konsum REIT AG
Ticker:	-
Sector:	Retail

Market Capitalization:	0.68 billion USD
Dividend Yield:	2.99%
Payout-Ratio:	37.85%

Country of Origin:	Germany
Core countries of investments:	Germany

Stability ✓
Diversification ✓
Yield ✓

Germany

Leverage Ratio: 54%

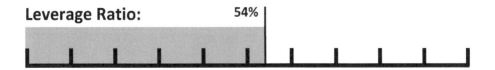

Kimco Realty Corp.[36]

Kimco is one of the largest retail REITs in the United States and a member of the S&P 500 stock exchange index. Regionally, it is limited to the east and West Coasts of the United States, Texas and in the north to some states around Chicago.

Its portfolio includes 420 properties and 47 million sf of retail space. It has "open-air" shopping centers, which, in contrast to covered malls, are distributed in individual buildings on a shopping area.

Kimco is involved in the purchase, development and management of shopping centers. The tenants of his buildings are retail chains for shopping, fashion, home furnishings and restaurants. So count e.g., Dunkin Donuts, Starbucks, Whole Foods Markets, CVS Pharmacy, Dollar Tree, Sprouts Farmers, Best Buy and Home Depot among its biggest customers.

But the portfolio is very broadly diversified, so only 14 tenants make up over 1% of sales. The largest of these with a maximum of 3.8%.

Kimco achieves growth by building new shopping centers. 27 further locations with 1,700,000 sf retail space are under development. Above many shopping centers, which are on the lower floors of a building, there are apartments with several hundred residential units that can be rented to private households.

Name:	Kimco Realty Corp.
Ticker:	KIM
Sector:	Retail
	Shopping Malls
Market Capitalization:	5.26 billion USD
Dividend Yield:	9.22%
Payout-Ratio:	89.23%
Country of Origin:	USA
Core countries of investments:	USA

Stability ✅
Diversification ✅
Yield ✅

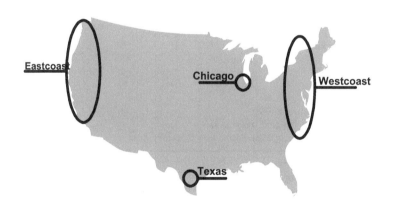

Leverage Ratio: 57%

Sources

26 Realty Income Corp.:
https://www.realtyincome.com/Home/default.aspx
https://www.realtyincome.com/portfolio/default.aspx
https://www.finanzen.net/aktien/realty-aktie
https://seekingalpha.com/symbol/O/dividends/scorecard?s=o

27 Simon Property Group Inc.:
https://investors.simon.com/
https://www.finanzen.net/aktien/simon_property_group-aktie
https://seekingalpha.com/symbol/SPG/dividends/scorecard?s=spg

28 National Retail Properties Inc.:
https://www.nnnreit.com/
https://www.nnnreit.com/properties-leasing/
https://www.finanzen.net/aktien/national_retail_properties-aktie
https://seekingalpha.com/symbol/NNN/dividends/scorecard?s=nnn

29 Tanger Factory Outlets Centers Inc.:
http://investors.tangeroutlet.com/
https://www.finanzen.net/aktien/tanger_factory_outlet_centers-aktie
https://seekingalpha.com/symbol/SKT
https://www.youtube.com/watch?v=0ujylfimOQQ

30 Gazit Globe Ltd.:
http://www.gazitglobe.com/
http://www.gazitglobe.com/properties/
https://www.finanzen.net/aktien/gazit_globe-aktie
https://seekingalpha.com/symbol/GZTGF/dividends/scorecard?s=gztgf

31 Link Real Estate Investment Trust:
https://www.linkreit.com/en/corporateProfile/
https://www.linkcorp.com/linkcorp/api/v1/file/SiteAssets/CorporateWebsite/InvestorRelat
ions/Presentations/201909%20Corporate%20Presentation%20(final).pdf?y=1f95954ef15
867f634c84d1158c3f91f
https://www.finanzen.net/aktien/link_real_estate_investment_trust-aktie

32 Fortune REIT:
https://www.fortunereit.com/html/about_profile.php
https://www.fortunereit.com/html/portfolio_map.php
https://www.finanzen.net/aktien/fortune_real_estate_investment_trust-aktie
33 Scentre Group:
https://www.scentregroup.com/investors/our-strategy
https://www.finanzen.net/aktien/scentre_group_stapled_security-aktie

34 Hamborner REIT AG:
https://www.hamborner.de/immobilien/uebersicht.html
https://www.hamborner.de/investor-relations/uebersicht.html
https://www.finanzen.net/aktien/hamborner_reit-aktie

35 Deutsche Konsum REIT AG:
https://www.deutsche-
konsum.de/fileadmin/content/investorrelations/praesentationen/DKR_Company_present
ation_12M_2017_2018_final.pdf
https://www.finanzen.net/aktien/deutsche_konsum_reit-aktie

36 Kimco Realty Corp.:
http://investors.kimcorealty.com/
http://properties.kimcorealty.com/property/output/find/search4/
https://seekingalpha.com/symbol/KIM/dividends/scorecard?s=kim
https://www.finanzen.net/aktien/kimco_realty-aktie

4.6   Industrial

Industrial REITs own industrial buildings such as department stores or logistics centers. Your tenants are always commercial customers who often come from trade, logistics or the manufacturing sector. Most REITs focus on logistics buildings such as warehouses or transshipment halls. However, the category also includes all other types of industrial buildings. Factories and halls in which products or intermediate products are manufactured, as well as specialized buildings such as Car dealerships belong to this category.

Depending on the industry, industrial REITs are heavily dependent on the economic situation. There is a strong demand for logistics halls, because internet trade is growing very rapidly and regularly requires expanded capacities. Almost every REIT fulfillment center from Amazon or parcel delivery companies such as UPS, FedEx or DHL are the largest tenants.

Warehouses can be built with little investment or know-how. Even if their location is easily accessible and near traffic junctions, the placement poses no further requirements. Entry barriers for competitors are, therefore, quite low. In times of good economic activity and strong demand, it often happens that many new buildings are built and come onto the market. This scenario is available and is fueled even further by the low interest rates. In this way, excess capacity arises and rental prices decrease because the supply increases. Should the economy weaken again, it may happen that vacancies and falling rents increase more than in other categories.

Since the industry is largely characterized by tenants who operate the logistics for e-commerce, the further development of the retail sector presents both opportunities and risks. If the retail trade and with it the necessary distribution of products and packages continues to grow, logistics REITs should benefit. However, shifts in purchasing behavior or new technologies can also put tenants' business models at risk. The effect of deliveries using drones or robots on the logistics industry is not yet foreseeable. Large internet retailers such as Amazon are also increasingly pushing into the market and covering more parts of the delivery itself. Classic REIT tenants can thus be pushed out of business. Too much concentration of a REIT on Amazon as the main tenant is also associated with risks and is not recommended. In an economic downturn, retailing is declining across the board, which should affect almost every REIT.

Duke Realty Corp.[37]

Duke Realty is a REIT that invests primarily in industrial warehouses and logistics centers. The buildings are primarily in the midwestern and southern United States.

The REIT owns, among other things, former General Motors factories, shipping centers for Amazon and buildings in a strategically important location around airports, ports and traffic hubs.

The portfolio comprises almost 161 million sf of usable space.

Duke Realty continues to offer services such as the development, construction and management of industrial buildings and is a broker for commercial space.

Name:	Duke Realty Corp.
Ticker:	DRE
Sector:	Distribution Centers

Market Capitalization:	13.26 billion USD
Dividend Yield:	2.64%
Payout-Ratio:	64.94%

Country of Origin:	USA
Core countries of investments:	USA

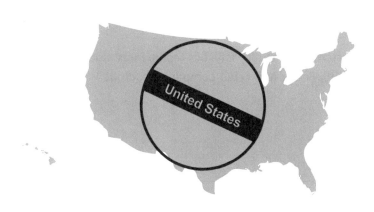

Stability ✔
Diversification ✔
Yield ✔

Leverage Ratio: 41%

Prologis Inc.[38]

Prologis is a REIT for commercial halls and logistics centers. The REIT operates throughout North and South America, as well as in Europe and Asia. It has 3,793 buildings with a total area of 796 million sf in 19 countries. Tenants are over 5,100 individual companies from the manufacturing, retail and transportation sectors. The company is one of the largest players in its field worldwide and has extensive expertise in the management of logistics properties. Prologis continues to conduct extensive market research and publish industry services „Industrial Business Indicator" and the "Prologis Logistics Rent Index".

The largest customers include logistics companies such as Amazon, UPS, DHL, FedEx and retail companies such as Home-Depot or Walmart.

Name:	Prologis Inc.
Ticker:	PLD
Sector:	Distribution Centers

Market Capitalization:	70.36 billion USD
Dividend Yield:	2.45%
Payout-Ratio:	64.61%

Country of Origin:	USA
Core countries of	USA
investments:	Europe
	Global

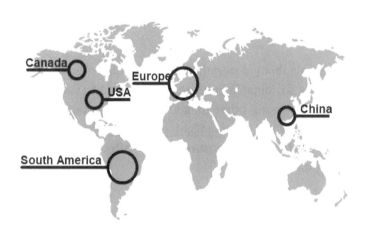

Leverage Ratio: 33%

Stag Industrial Inc.[39]

Stag Industrial is a broad-based industrial REIT diversified in various industries, regions and tenant groups. His department stores and logistics centers are spread across tenants from over 45 industries and over 60 regional markets. No single market has a share of over 10% in the overall portfolio and no single tenant is larger than 2%.

The portfolio comprises 86 million sf usable space in 430 buildings.

The REIT focuses on profitable investments with low risk, tenants with good credit ratings and pursues both internal growth through steady rent increases and external growth through new acquisitions.

Through various sustainability programs, Stag Industrial tries to be perceived both as a sustainable building operator and to save on maintenance costs. Among other things, Solar cells installed on the roofs of the buildings, and sunlight-absorbing materials and more economical lighting ensure more effective air conditioning and lighting.

Name:	Stag Industrial Inc.
Ticker:	STAG
Sector:	Distribution Centers

Market Capitalization:	4.36 billion USD
Dividend Yield:	4.97%
Payout-Ratio:	78.29%

Country of Origin:	USA
Core countries of investments:	USA

Leverage Ratio: 45%

Gladstone Commercial Corp.[40]

Gladstone Commercial is an industrial REIT from the United States. He has a portfolio with an area of 13 million sf of office buildings, warehouses, archives and factories. In contrast to many other industrial REITs, Gladstone has more factories and production buildings and not exclusively distribution centers or logistics halls. The REIT is, therefore, suitable for diversification in the industrial sector.

109 commercial properties are rented to 101 companies in 24 countries, mainly in the eastern United States. The REIT focuses on properties in prime locations, in growing submarkets with a stable property value.

Gladstone rents its buildings to individual tenants, e.g., General Motors or other suppliers to the automotive industry, but also to several tenants who share one property. A total of 19 sectors are represented among the tenants.

The REIT never cut or canceled its dividend to shareholders and continued paying it even in the financial crisis.

Name:	Gladstone Commercial Corp.
Ticker:	GOOD
Sector:	Industrial Factories Distribution Centers
Market Capitalization:	0.62 billion USD
Dividend Yield:	6.74%
Payout-Ratio:	77.62%
Country of Origin:	USA
Core countries of investments:	USA

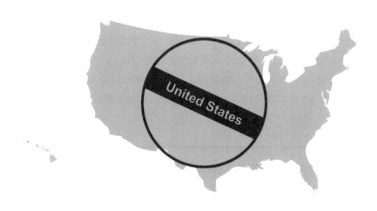

Leverage Ratio: 66%

Innovative Industrial Properties Inc.[41]

Innovative Industrial Properties is the first REIT to specialize in cannabis-growing buildings.

With the legalization of cannabis in many U.S. states, many companies have emerged that need financing solutions for a quick start in this new industry.

Innovative Industrial quickly took advantage of this opportunity and began in 2016 to buy cannabis companies' production halls on long-term contracts or to build them for them to optimize their capital requirements. The largest REIT has emerged in the cannabis industry.

The REIT is an interesting alternative to the very fluctuating, pure cannabis stocks. It is also profitable right from the start and pays a dividend. This cannot be expected from cannabis stocks unless the market is consolidated and the legal situation is more stable.

So far there are only a few competing companies with a comparable investment approach, e.g., the companies Power REIT, Freehold Properties or RealCanna.

Since the cannabis market is still very young and is subject to extremely strong political influence, the REIT is a riskier investment despite its previous successes. The likelihood of cannabis legalization failing or cannabis companies going bankrupt is significantly higher than in other industries.

Name:	Innovative Industrial Properties Inc.
Ticker:	IIPR
Sector:	Production Halls for growing Cannabis

Market Capitalization:	1.99 billion USD
Dividend Yield:	4.62%
Payout-Ratio:	88.43%

Country of Origin:	USA
Core countries of investments:	USA

Stability
Diversification
Yield

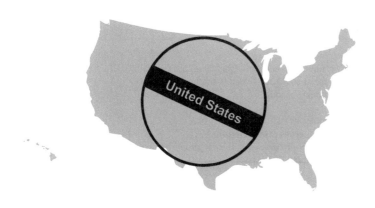

20%

Leverage Ratio:

Sources

37 Duke Realty Corp.:
https://www.dukerealty.com/who-we-are/why-duke-realty/
https://www.finanzen.net/aktien/duke_realty-aktie
https://seekingalpha.com/symbol/DRE/dividends/scorecard?s=dre

38 Prologis Inc.:
https://www.prologis.com/about
https://ir.prologis.com/investor-overview/default.aspx
https://www.finanzen.net/aktien/prologis-aktie
https://seekingalpha.com/symbol/PLD/dividends/scorecard?s=pld

39 Stag Industrial Inc.:
http://ir.stagindustrial.com/Cache/1001258431.PDF?O=PDF&T=&Y=&D=&FID=100125843
1&iid=4263385
https://www.stagindustrial.com/
https://www.finanzen.net/aktien/stag_industrial-aktie

40 Gladstone Commercial Corp.:
https://ir.gladstonecommercial.com/static-files/66304050-8ebd-4121-8691-
1a9ff2b49114
https://www.gladstonecommercial.com/
https://www.finanzen.net/unternehmensprofil/gladstone_commercial
https://seekingalpha.com/symbol/GOOD/dividends/scorecard?s=good
https://www.gladstonecommercial.com/

41 Innovative Industrial Properties Inc.:
http://innovativeindustrialproperties.com/our-business/
https://www.finanzen.net/aktien/innovative_industrial_properties-aktie
https://seekingalpha.com/symbol/IIPR?s=iipr

4.7 Datacenter[42]

Datacenter REITs own and manage buildings in which customers store servers to store their data. REITs for data centers offer a range of products and services to ensure the security of servers and data. These include uninterruptible power supplies, air-cooled chillers, and physical security and access controls.

In the form of a REIT, the REIT owns the property, the building and the building infrastructure such as energy supply, cooling and connections to internet connections. The REIT provides parking spaces, cabinets and cages for servers within the buildings. The servers themselves are brought by the respective customers and maintained, installed and kept up to date on their own account. The investment risk of a REIT regarding outdated technologies is, therefore, relatively low and rather shifted to the customer. But regular investments in security and connection connections are necessary. However, these can be planned and are factored into rental contracts and investment plans.

Opportunities arise from the increasing demand for services that process and store data. Current trends such as autonomous driving, Internet of Things, virtual reality and artificial intelligence require incredible resources to process the resulting data. According to the common opinion, these developments are only just beginning, so that an extremely strong increase in demand should be expected. Companies that offer these services rely on rapid growth. This conflicts with the high-cost one

Bring investment in data centers and related technology. In addition, data centers must be physically close to internet nodes to achieve a fast and trouble-free connection. Data centers that meet these criteria can, therefore, not be built anywhere and in infinite numbers. Datacenter REITs take advantage of this because they have occupied most of the nodes and are in a good starting position to react to the developing trends.

Risks for data center REITs are less foreseeable than with other categories. There are currently no reasons for declining demand. However, as new technologies become more widespread and more and more data can be stored in less and less space, prices can drop.

There are also security risks if a REIT repeatedly reveals security gaps in its systems or if data centers could be hacked. This could cause considerable damage to the image.

Due to the limited number of possible data centers on an internet node, only a few new data centers can be built. It is more likely that the industry will consolidate. REITs can grow faster if they simply buy up competitors. But this can also lead to an increase in debt.

Risks can be seen in the overvaluation of data center REITs. This category has risen sharply due to its positive future expectations. The ratings are significantly higher than other REITs and are more similar to that of technology companies. This category also has a significantly lower dividend yield relative to the price.

Digital Realty Trust Inc.[43]

Digital Realty is the leading infrastructure REIT in the data center category.

It is the 9th largest REIT in the United States and a member of the S&P 500 stock exchange index.

The REIT owns buildings for data centers and their technical infrastructure and creates a reliable and secure environment for server storage. He operates the security, cooling, data connection and energy supply. However, the actual servers are owned by the tenants. The REIT is, therefore, not affected by the technology and investment risk of the servers.

The data center REIT category is benefiting greatly from the cloud boom. Statistics expect strong growth in the areas of Internet of Things, artificial intelligence, autonomous driving and virtual reality. This trend will further support the demand for data centers.

Digital Realty generates growth by buying data centers from companies and leasing them back to them. The tenants, e.g., In this way, large mobile operators and large corporations streamline their balance sheets and uncover liquidity. Customers can rent individual cabinets or large packages for their servers.

Digital Realty owns 210 data centers in 14 countries. These include the United States, Germany, Japan, China, Australia, Singapore, Brazil and all of Europe. Its data centers total 33 million sf of rental space.

Name:	Digital Realty Trust Inc.
Ticker:	DLR
Sector:	Datacenter

Market Capitalization:	40.82 billion USD
Dividend Yield:	3.04%
Payout-Ratio:	75.42%

Country of Origin:	USA
Core countries of	USA
investments:	Global

Stability ✓
Diversification ✓
Yield ✓

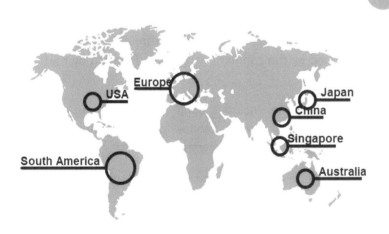

Leverage Ratio: 48%

Equinix Inc.[44]

Equinix is an American REIT that offers network-independent data centers and interconnections as services. The company is active in forty countries and offers its customers space in its data centers as well as direct connections to network operators and other companies within the data center, so-called interconnections.

In addition, there are numerous large internet nodes in the Equinix data centers. Equinix sees these internet nodes, at the location of which it is strategically positioned, the decisive key to future success. These internet nodes are of crucial importance for operating the global data exchange. Proximity and preferred access to these nodes offer business benefits and faster connection for customers. Such nodes cannot easily be relocated, occupied by the competition or manufactured by the competition.

Equinix's customer base includes large and medium-sized companies, in particular cloud service providers, financial companies, internet retailers and network operators.

Equinix data centers can be found in the United States, throughout Europe, Asia and South America. A total of 204 data centers are spread across 25 countries.

Name:	Digital Realty Trust Inc.
Ticker:	DLR
Sector:	Datacenter

Market Capitalization:	40.82 billion USD
Dividend Yield:	3.04%
Payout-Ratio:	75.42%

Country of Origin:	USA
Core countries of	USA
investments:	Global

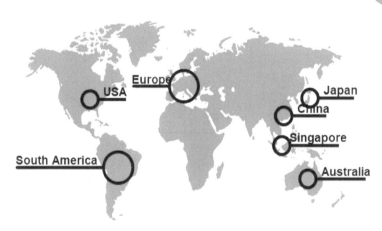

Leverage Ratio: 48%

CoreSite Realty Corp.[45]

CoreSite is a REIT specializing in data center buildings.

He operates data centers with a usable area of 4.5 million sf for 1,350 customers. It has 23 data centers in 49 states.

The REIT sees itself well protected against competition due to high entry barriers. The most important data traffic hubs are now occupied by the data center operators. It takes a long time and high investments to build new centers. A consolidation in the industry may still follow.

Name:	CoreSite Realty Corp.
Ticker:	COR
Sector:	Datacenter

Market Capitalization:	5.97 billion USD
Dividend Yield:	3.98%
Payout-Ratio:	94.68%

Country of Origin:	USA
Core countries of investments:	USA

Stability ✓
Diversification ✓
Yield ✓

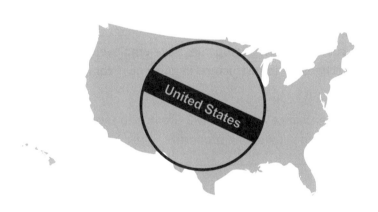

Leverage Ratio: 92%

CyrusOne Inc.[46]

CyrusOne is a data center REIT from the United States. It operates 45 data centers in North America, Asia, Europe and South America.

Its tenants are around 1000 companies, of the top Fortune 1000 companies, 200 are customers at Cyrus One.

As it grows, the REIT focuses on companies that want to outsource their IT infrastructure and offers them extensive services to optimize their balance sheet and liquidity. For this purpose, the servers are moved from the companies to the CyrusOne data centers. There they can be managed more efficiently and cost-effectively. Companies save employees and the necessary technology infrastructure in their own company buildings.

Wikipedia and the exchange operator CME Group also save their data on servers housed in CyrusOne properties.

Name:	CyrusOne Inc.
Ticker:	CONE
Sector:	Datacenter

Market Capitalization:	8.79 billion USD
Dividend Yield:	2.62%
Payout-Ratio:	52.10%

Country of Origin:	USA
Core countries of	USA
investments:	Global

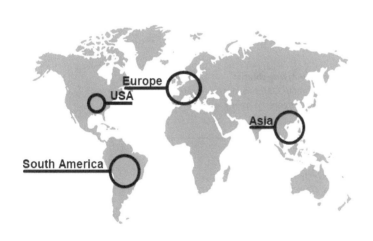

Leverage Ratio: 62%

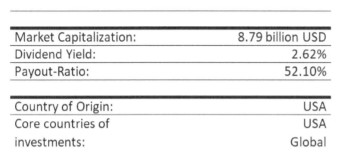

Sources

42 Datencenter
https://money.usnews.com/investing/investing-101/articles/why-data-center-reits-are-promising-and-risky

43 Digital Realty Trust Inc.:
https://www.digitalrealty.com/about
https://investor.digitalrealty.com/overview/investor-relations-overview/default.aspx
https://s22.q4cdn.com/864880006/files/doc_presentations/2019/11/NAREIT-2019-Investor-Presentation-vF.pdf
https://www.digitalrealty.de/data-center-solutions
https://www.finanzen.net/aktien/digital_realty_trust-aktie
https://seekingalpha.com/symbol/DLR/dividends/scorecard?s=dlr

44 Equinix Inc.:
https://www.equinix.com/data-centers/
https://www.equinix.com/about/
http://investor.equinix.com/static-files/e35fe6c2-e62a-4d5a-ae20-d3f07e04ccef
https://investor.equinix.com/phoenix.zhtml?c=122662&p=irol-irhome
https://www.finanzen.net/aktien/equinix_1-aktie
https://seekingalpha.com/symbol/EQIX/dividends/scorecard?s=eqix

45 CoreSite Realty Corp.:
https://www.coresite.com/about/why-coresite
https://seekingalpha.com/symbol/COR/dividends/scorecard?s=cor
https://www.finanzen.net/aktien/coresite_realty-aktie

46 CyrusOne Inc.:
https://cyrusone.com/about/
http://investor.cyrusone.com/
https://www.finanzen.net/aktien/cyrusone-aktie
https://seekingalpha.com/symbol/CONE/dividends/scorecard?s=cone

4.8   Storage

Storage REITs include all types of buildings that are suitable for storing items. The most common type among REITs are self-storage warehouses, in which customers store their household items independently.

In the United States, people are much more mobile and move more often. In order not to always take the whole household with them, they often store parts of their household goods until they move back again.

Most storage rooms can be set up with little know-how and with no special technical features. Depending on the type of storage, lighting, heating or other infrastructure of a normal building can be saved. The location of a storage warehouse does not have to be too exclusive, as with many other properties of other categories. Good accessibility is more important, i.e., often a central location near a motorway. The entry barriers for standard self-storage properties are, therefore, rather low. This is also noticeable in the increasing saturation of the American market.

Special bearings promise higher chances and a lower risk. Such bearings often meet special temperature and climate requirements. Valuable objects or works of art, but also musical instruments, wine or items made from sensitive materials can be stored in them. For this type of warehouse, competition is less, entry barriers are higher and warehouse rent promises a higher share of profits.

If customers cannot pay their rent, it is common for the Storage-REIT to exercise its lien and auction the stored items.

Public Storage[47]

Public Storage is the oldest and largest REIT in the Storage category and comes from the United States. The REIT is a member of the S&P 500 stock exchange index.

The REIT owns nearly 2,500 properties in the United States and 193 in Europe. These comprise 170 million sf of storage space. For the Canadian market, the trademark rights were sold against payment of a license.

The REIT offers its customers storage space for storing personal or commercial items. Other sources of income come from the sale of packaging material and moving boxes.

Public storage also includes special buildings, e.g., Car dealerships or buildings that meet special climatic conditions.

Public Storage has highly automated access to its storage rooms, so the REIT needs only a minimum of personnel.

Public Storage continues to own 42% of PS Business Parks Inc., an office park company and a member of the S&P MidCap 400.

Name:	Public Storage
Ticker:	PSA
Sector:	Self Storage

Market Capitalization:	34.04 billion USD
Dividend Yield:	4.11%
Payout-Ratio:	75.98%

Country of Origin:	USA
Core countries of	USA
investments:	Europe

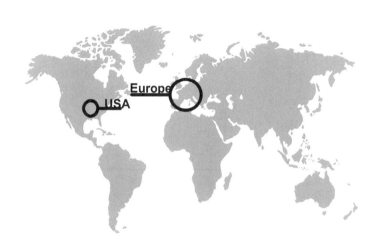

Leverage Ratio:

24%

Big Yellow Group Plc.[48]

Big Yellow is the UK's largest self-storage REIT. The REIT operates 92 properties in which there are storage rooms for private individuals, students and corporate customers.

Big Yellow offers 20 sizes for storage rooms: from cloakroom lockers to entire warehouses. Units that can be driven by a car or parking spaces for storing your own containers are also possible. All storage rooms have individual alarm systems.

The name Big Yellow refers to the size and color of the buildings, which are painted in yellow and can be seen from afar. The Big Yellow name has become synonymous with the whole self-storage industry in the UK.

Name:	Big Yellow Group Plc.
Ticker:	BYLOF
Sector:	Self Storage

Market Capitalization:	2.19 billion USD
Dividend Yield:	3.02%
Payout-Ratio:	82.50%

Country of Origin:	UK
Core countries of investments:	UK

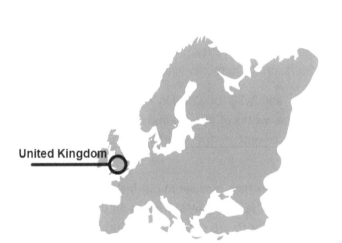

United Kingdom

28%

Leverage Ratio:

Iron Mountain Inc.[49]

Iron Mountain is an American REIT that specializes in data storage buildings for businesses.

After the end of the cold war, Iron Mountain bought out old bunker systems and converted them so they could serve as permanent and safe stores of all kinds.

Large corporations and medium-sized companies mainly store company data and files in 1,500 REIT warehouses worldwide. Professional document shredding is also carried out. Iron Mountain guarantees individual storage for particularly sensitive data and objects - among other things in the bunker systems mentioned. This means that warehouses with an increased security status and permanent security, but also with special requirements for temperature or humidity, can be offered.

Iron Mountain's estates and wills of Charles Darwin, Charles Dickens and Princess Diana, works of art, original recordings and films of famous works are kept in the Iron Mountain stores worldwide.

Although the storage of paper files may seem old-fashioned, an incredibly high proportion of the economy still relies on this type of document management. There are often statutory retention requirements of many years that can be met efficiently via Iron Mountains services. Iron Mountain faces the ravages of time by founding a new business unit for cloud services and data centers.

Name:	Iron Mountain Inc.
Ticker:	IRM
Sector:	Archives Datacenter
Market Capitalization:	7.50 billion USD
Dividend Yield:	9.50%
Payout-Ratio:	117.06%
Country of Origin:	USA
Core countries of investments:	USA Global

Stability ✓
Diversification ✓
Yield ✓

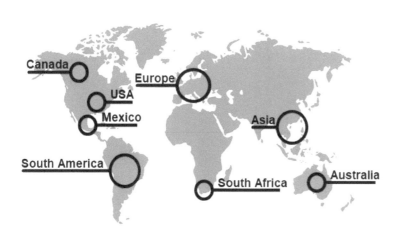

Leverage Ratio: 91%

Sources

47 Public Storage
https://www.publicstorage.com/our-story
https://www.finanzen.net/aktien/public_storage_1-aktie
https://seekingalpha.com/symbol/PSA/dividends/scorecard?s=psa

48 Big Yellow Group Plc.:
https://www.bigyellow.co.uk/
https://www.finanzen.net/aktien/big_yellow_group-aktie
https://seekingalpha.com/symbol/BYLOF/dividends/scorecard?s=bylof

49 Iron Mountain Inc.:
https://www.ironmountain.com/about-us
https://www.finanzen.net/aktien/iron_mountain_1-aktie
https://seekingalpha.com/symbol/IRM/dividends/scorecard?s=irm

4.9 Prisons

The prison REITs industry is very small and only US REITs can be found. There are only two listed companies in which small investors can participate. The remaining companies are owned by private equity firms.

The special properties of prison REITs can include all types of facilities with an increased security status. The most common types of property are prisons.

But there are also refugee camps illegally in the country. They are cared for in these camps until their legal status is established and immigration is approved or rejected.

As a rule, leases and concessions are agreed with public authorities on a long-term basis. Due to high entry hurdles and massively necessary investments in security, the business model can only be copied poorly by competitors.

On the other hand, the private prisons and refugee camps sector has recently been exposed to various negative reports. The conditions under which inmates have to live are repeatedly criticized. Private prisons were also an issue in the last US election campaign. It is precisely the Democratic presidential candidates who are campaigning against the privatization of facilities such as prisons. The industry is, therefore, heavily dependent on the political landscape.

The Geo Group Inc.[50]

Geo Group is an American prison REIT. His investments are limited to buildings for public institutions with high-security status, such as prisons, detention centers and psychiatric hospitals. Refugee homes and initial reception centers are also operated for the US government. Prisons account for 45% of the total portfolio.

The REIT's buildings are in the United States, Great Britain, South Africa and Australia. 81,000 inmates are looked after in 118 institutions.

Geo Group has benefited from privatization in the United States and has bought many buildings from the government. The REIT rents some buildings to the respective prison operators, who are still state or federal authorities. However, facilities with their own staff are operated themselves.

Besides ownership, Geo Group is also involved in the construction and planning of facilities and offers various services for government organizations. These include transport services with their own high-security vehicles and the administration of ankle cuffs for criminals.

Name:	The Geo Group Inc.
Ticker:	GEO
Sector:	Prisons
	Refugee Camps

Market Capitalization:	1.37 billion USD
Dividend Yield:	16.71%
Payout-Ratio:	208.70%

Country of Origin:	USA
Core countries of	USA
investments:	UK, South Africa,
	Australia

Stability ⊘
Diversification ✓
Yield ✓

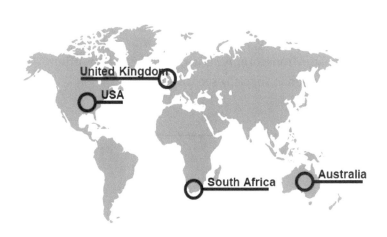

Leverage Ratio: 77%

CoreCivic Inc.[51]

CoreCivic is an American REIT that specializes in the construction, operation and management of private prisons.

The company operates over 70 institutions in the United States, many of which are owned and the rest as tenants or tenants.

Approximately 90,000 inmates are looked after.

Besides pure prisons, others are also working on construction, government buildings, refugee camps and residential centers for rehabilitation. As part of re-socialization programs, CoreCivic offers comprehensive education programs for its inmates to enable them to receive training and prepare them for a life without crime.

With its subsidiary Transcore America, the REIT also offers prisoner transportation in specially secured vehicles

Name:	CoreCivic Inc.
Ticker:	CXW
Sector:	Prisons
	Refugee Camps

Market Capitalization:	1.10 billion USD
Dividend Yield:	-
Payout-Ratio:	-

Country of Origin:	USA
Core countries of investments:	USA

Stability
Diversification
Yield

Leverage Ratio: 66%

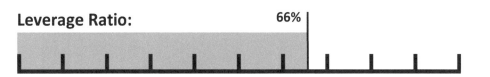

Sources

50 The Geo Group Inc.:
https://www.geogroup.com/who_we_are
https://www.finanzen.net/aktien/the_geo_group_1-aktie
https://seekingalpha.com/symbol/GEO/dividends/scorecard?s=geo

51 CoreCivic Inc.:
http://www.corecivic.com/about
https://www.finanzen.net/aktien/corecivic-aktie
https://seekingalpha.com/symbol/CXW/dividends/scorecard?s=cxw

4.10 Land

Agricultural REITs focus largely on agricultural land and land. Their value is more on the land than on the buildings erected on it.

But many agricultural areas are designed for a specific type of fruit permanently grown on them. With orchards, vineyards or forest land, the stock of trees and perennials can be viewed as a property. Like a property, these plants are subject to a decline in current value and must be replanted or maintained consistently.

In forest areas (English: "Timber") forests are held as an investment. Since many houses in the USA are still made of wood, wood is an important building material and, therefore, dependent on economic fluctuations in industry and the prices of construction wood.

With proper care and management, both forest and agricultural areas can be very valuable and stable in price. Agricultural areas for food supply should benefit from population growth and increasing food shortages.

However, the industry is also at risk from natural disasters such as forest fires, floods and droughts. However, it can also benefit from those if it is not itself affected and can fill the gaps in supply resulting from disasters.

Weyerhaeuser Co.[52]

Weyerhaeuser is a REIT in the category Timber REITs. So she invests in forest land. The REIT has existed since 1900 and is the largest private forest owner in the world.

Most of its land is in the United States, but is otherwise invested worldwide. The forest area in the USA alone is 53,668 square miles. In Canada, the REIT manages the same area of rented forest again.

Weyerhaeuser operates along the entire timber management chain. The REIT has its own forests and sells wood as a material and as finished products. We also operate our own sawmills. Land is developed into building land and residential houses are built from their own material, which are then sold. In addition, the REIT is active in energy supply by selling wood pellets as an energy source and operating solar cells and wind farms on its own property.

Minerals are also mined on the property and seeds and fertilizers are sold to external customers. In some forest areas, recreational activities such as hiking, hunting and fishing are even offered to generate additional income from the forest property.

Name:	Weyerhaeuser Co.
Ticker:	WY
Sector:	Timberland

Market Capitalization:	16.57 billion USD
Dividend Yield:	6.13%
Payout-Ratio:	668.11%

Country of Origin:	USA
Core countries of	USA
investments:	Canada

Leverage Ratio: 53%

Rayonier Inc.[53]

Rayonier is a Timber REIT that holds forests in the United States and, through a joint venture, also in New Zealand in its portfolio. It has 4,000 square miles of forest area, including approximately 2,800 square miles in the south of the United States in Florida, Georgia and Alabama and 580 in the north and in the Pacific region.

Rayonier was originally founded as a paper mill and, after World War II, bought up massive forests in the northeastern United States.

The REIT has an extremely long-term planning horizon, so processed wood stocks are consistently reforested. Sometimes, however, land is also converted into building plots and sold.

Rayonier generates additional income by leasing land to hunters and beekeepers and leaving it to operators of solar parks, wind energy and radio masts.

Firewood and biomass are produced and sold from the forest. Soils such as minerals, sand, oil and gas are mined and sold on areas that cannot be farmed productively.

Name:	Rayonier Inc.
Ticker:	RYN
Sector:	Timberland

Market Capitalization:	3.16 billion USD
Dividend Yield:	4.41%
Payout-Ratio:	712.54%

Country of Origin:	USA
Core countries of	USA
investments:	New Zealand

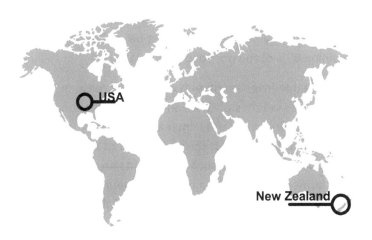

Leverage Ratio: 49%

Farmland Partners Inc.[54]

Farmland Partners is a REIT for arable land and agricultural land. The REIT owns the land and the fields and rents them out to farmers who cultivate it on their own account. The portfolio includes properties in 17 US states, valued at USD 1.2 billion, on which 30 types of plants are grown.

The properties consist of fields, plantations, tree nurseries and vines and cover a total area of 625 square miles. They are used to grow apples, wine, almonds, avocado, rice, corn and other cereals. Approximately 20% of the portfolio is overgrown with trees that can be viewed as a building. Like real estate, they need permanent care and maintenance and must be replaced in old age. The remaining 80% of the portfolio is pure land.

Arable land is a very stable investment with a steady increase in value and low price losses in times of crisis. Since the population and the need for food are constantly increasing, agriculture hardly knows any drop in demand. But the yield depends on the raw material prices. Natural disasters such as droughts are also a problem, but the farmers bear the main entrepreneurial risk. The industrialization of agriculture increases the profitability of agriculture. Farmland Partners benefit from this trend without having to take the investment risk for agricultural machinery etc. The farmer pays for this purchase, but the REIT can always demand higher leases. The REIT manages this portfolio with only 15-20 employees.

Name:	Farmland Partners Inc.
Ticker:	FPI
Sector:	Farmland
	Plantations
	Vineyards
Market Capitalization:	0.20 billion USD
Dividend Yield:	3.03%
Payout-Ratio:	35.93%
Country of Origin:	USA
Core countries of	USA
investments:	

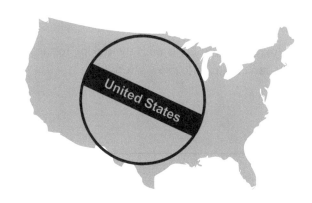

Leverage Ratio: 49%

Gladstone Land Corp.[55]

Gladstone Land is a REIT that specializes in agricultural land. His portfolio includes fields and plantations on which various types of fruit and cereals are grown. The most important cultivars include apples, cherries, blueberries, strawberries, corn and cereals.

The properties are in several states in the United States: Arizona, California, Colorado, Florida, Michigan, Nebraska, North Carolina, Oregon and Washington.

Compared to other REITs, Gladstone is rather small. Its market capitalization is just around USD

357 million. However, the REIT is actively looking for acquisition properties so it can continue to grow strongly.

Name:	Gladstone Land Corp.
Ticker:	LAND
Sector:	Farmland Plantations

Market Capitalization:	0.33 billion USD
Dividend Yield:	3.47%
Payout-Ratio:	78.26%

Country of Origin:	USA
Core countries of investments:	USA

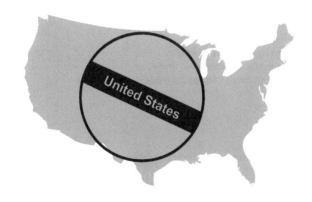

Leverage Ratio: 63%

Sources

52 Weyerhaeuser Company:
https://www.weyerhaeuser.com/timberlands/
https://www.finanzen.net/aktien/weyerhaeuser-aktie
https://seekingalpha.com/symbol/WY/dividends/scorecard?s=wy

53 Rayonier Inc.:
https://www.rayonier.com/our-businesses/forestry/
https://www.rayonier.com/about-us/company-snapshot/
https://www.finanzen.net/aktien/rayonier_1-aktie
https://seekingalpha.com/symbol/RYN?s=ryn

54 Farmland Partners Inc.:
http://www.farmlandpartners.com/about-us/
http://www.farmlandpartners.com/properties/
https://www.finanzen.net/aktien/farmland_partners-aktie
https://seekingalpha.com/symbol/FPI/dividends/scorecard?s=fpi

55 Gladstone Land Corp.:
https://gladstonefarms.com/
https://gladstonefarms.com/farmland-portfolio/
https://www.finanzen.net/aktien/gladstone_land-aktie
https://seekingalpha.com/symbol/LAND/dividends/scorecard?s=land

4.11 Infrastructure

Infrastructure is understood to mean the basic equipment of an economy as well as basic services provided for the population as a whole. While infrastructure was almost exclusively financed by the state in the past, more state-owned companies and infrastructure projects have been privatized or financed externally due to the high level of investment and tight government budgets. Some investors take advantage of this and founded the category of infrastructure REITs.

For REITs, however, only infrastructures related to a building or a property can be considered. The REIT often owns the property only under a certain type of infrastructure and does not operate it itself.

Investments in REITs are, therefore, often limited to the categories of telecommunications infrastructure (e.g., radio towers and fiber optic cables) as well as petrol stations or pipelines.

Other types of infrastructure, e.g., Roads, water supply and disposal are not buildings and, therefore, cannot benefit from the tax-privileged legal form of the REITs.

Competition for REITs arises less from spatial competition, but rather from displacement by other technologies. Infrastructure investments depend often on the technological change that affects the respective category. Technical infrastructure such as radio towers in the future could be replaced by satellite-based internet connections.

But a strategically advantageous location can offer opportunities in growth and demographic Development of the surrounding population. For example, certain regions can have population growth or just have access to certain technologies.

Infrastructure is almost always subject to a high level of government influence, since the services offered are essential for the population. High regulations and regulations generate high costs for operating infrastructure. In return, however, binding remuneration is often given so the desired infrastructure is even offered in weak regions.

American Tower Corp.[56]

American Tower (AMT) is a REIT that specializes in infrastructure for the communications industry. His investments mainly include radio towers and the associated properties, which are rented to mobile phone companies. Antennas, cables, ticket booths and other infrastructure required for operation belong to the operators and are installed and maintained at their expense.

American Tower has 171,000 radio towers, including 41,000 in the United States and approximately 2,200 in Germany. Overall, AMT is active in 17 countries and has expanded its presence in rapidly growing countries such as Mexico, several South American countries, France, India and some African countries.

The company benefits from both a rapidly increasing amount of data in industrialized countries and the increasing spread of basic smartphones in developing countries. The demand for mobile data and the necessary infrastructure is increasing in both areas. American Tower believes it is well positioned in developing countries to benefit from their adjustments to the latest data standards. It is estimated that developing countries and emerging economies in 5 years will have data sales like those in developed countries. AMT will then already be the dominant player and have the critical infrastructure.

Name:	American Tower Corp.
Ticker:	AMT
Sector:	Communication Towers

Stability ✓
Diversification ✓
Yield ✓

Market Capitalization:	117.91 billion USD
Dividend Yield:	1.65%
Payout-Ratio:	56.25%

Country of Origin:	USA
Core countries of investments:	USA
	Global

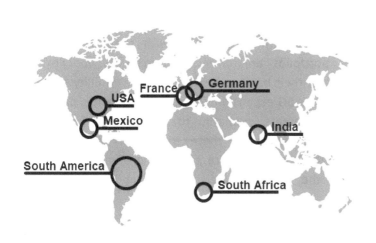

Leverage Ratio: 88%

SBA Communications Corp.[57]

SBA Communications is an infrastructure REIT with radio towers and antenna masts. His investments focus on North and South America and South Africa.

The REIT earns its income by renting and building radio towers and by installing equipment on them. SBA also operates cell phone systems on rooftops in city centers. In total, the REIT manages over 38,000 units on its own or rented land. SBA rents land from private individuals, land or house owners, installs its own towers and rents them to several mobile phone companies that install their antennas on them.

The REIT grows primarily through acquisitions and buys both individual towers and entire portfolios with thousands of towers. These portfolios are often outsourced by mobile operators to protect their balance sheet or to raise liquidity for other projects such as 5G expansion. Particular attention is paid to the emerging markets, primarily to Central and South America. The infrastructure in these markets is still less developed, but mobile networks are gaining more weight and dynamism than the use of fixed networks in developing countries.

Name:	SBA Communications Corp.
Ticker:	SBAC
Sector:	Communication Towers

Market Capitalization:	34.10 billion USD
Dividend Yield:	0.61%
Payout-Ratio:	28.39%

Country of Origin:	USA
Core countries of	USA
investments:	Global

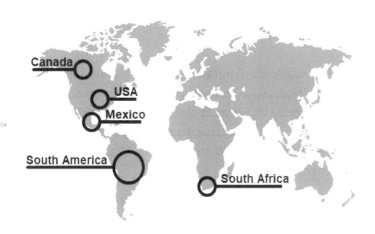

Canada

USA

Mexico

South America

South Africa

Leverage Ratio: 145%

Uniti Group Inc.[58]

Uniti belongs to the group of communication infrastructure REITs. His activity extends to the ownership and construction of radio towers (towers) and fiber optic cables (fiber). Within the United States, the REIT owns 2.1 million km of fiber optic cables, and a further 4.9 million km are leased to corporate customers. The radio towers division has 683 radio masts. Unitis Investments cover approximately the eastern half of the United States.

In the Uniti area, 4G and 5G penetration is still very low. Uniti, therefore, expects strong growth in this division. The REIT is characterized by further growth in Mexico, a dynamic market growing rapidly and still has a lot of potential for expanding technical infrastructure.

The market for communication infrastructure has extremely high barriers to entry because a competitor could hardly build the necessary infrastructure in terms of form and the market is highly regulated. Mobile operators are extremely dependent on the infrastructure operated by Uniti to serve their customers and cannot easily change locations.

Uniti continues to provide services for telecom companies and assembles, installs and maintains the antennas mounted on the radio towers. For broader regional coverage, rooftops from other owners are also rented and radio towers are installed on them.

Name:	Uniti Group Inc.
Ticker:	UNIT
Sector:	Communication Towers Fiber

Market Capitalization:	1.85 billion USD
Dividend Yield:	6.11%
Payout-Ratio:	57.94%

Country of Origin:	USA
Core countries of investments:	USA Mexico

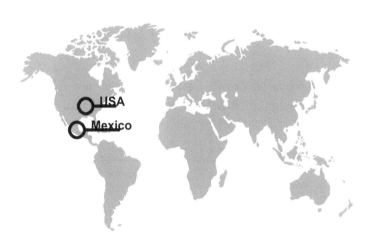

Leverage Ratio: 132%

Crown Castle International Corp.[59]

Crown Castle is an infrastructure REIT telecommunications industry. In contrast to many REITS in its category, it not only has around 40,000 radio towers but also 120,000 km of fiber optic cables and 70,000 so-called small cells. Small cells are small cell phone antennas with a range of up to 200 m. They can be installed at high-traffic locations on lampposts, traffic lights, parking columns or house facades and secure the data connection for the next generation of 5G, Internet of Things, self-driving cars and smart cities.

All investments are in the United States. They are rented to cell phone companies that provide mobile data and cell phones for their customers.

Bill Gates has also discovered Crown Castle's potential and is involved in the REIT through a Bill & Melinda Gates foundation with 5.3 million shares.

Name:	Crown Castle International Corp.
Ticker:	CCI
Sector:	Communication Towers Fiber Small Cells
Market Capitalization:	71.48 billion USD
Dividend Yield:	2.80%
Payout-Ratio:	82.16%
Country of Origin:	USA
Core countries of investments:	USA

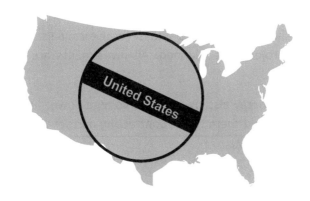

Leverage Ratio: 74%

CorEnergy Infrastructure Trust Inc.[60]

CorEnergy is the only REIT that specializes in investments in the energy industry. His facilities include pipelines, tanks, and handling terminals for the oil and gas industry. Energy companies rent the systems on long-term contracts. The maintenance and repair obligation as well as regular rent increases for the tenant are determined by means of triple net agreements.

CorEnergy focuses on long-term, strategically located investments vital for the business of its customers and have high entry barriers.

CorEnergy owns gas pipelines, gas processing and storage facilities, offshore oil pipelines and several terminals. Further construction projects are planned. All investments are in the United States.

In the past, CorEnergy also owned high-voltage power lines and substations, but sold them to the contracting partner at the end of the leasing contract.

Name:	CorEnergy Infrastructure Trust Inc.
Ticker:	CORR
Sector:	Pipelines Gas-Terminals
Market Capitalization:	0.11 billion USD
Dividend Yield:	2.57%
Payout-Ratio:	45.45%
Country of Origin:	USA
Core countries of investments:	USA

Stability ✓
Diversification ✓
Yield ✓

Leverage Ratio: 36%

Getty Realty Corp.[61]

Getty Realty is a REIT that owns, leases, and funds gas stations. The REIT was created as a spin-off of the oil company Getty Oil. Its portfolio includes 936 gas stations with associated shops located in 33 states in the United States. The properties are in the United States with the highest population density, mainly in the East, West and South of the United States.

The tenants of the buildings are almost all well-known, large chains of mineral oil companies such as Getty, BP, Shell and Exxon Mobil.

Petrol stations are an irreplaceable building block in the infrastructure of a population. A REIT like Getty, who owns buildings in a strategically important location, can be sure of continued demand. Cars also must be charged and repaired in the event of a change in mobility, away from oil and towards electromobility.

Petrol stations are rented using the triple net lease method. With this, the tenant pays for all maintenance costs himself. This includes taxes, maintenance, repairs, insurance and all operating costs, such as personnel and crude oil costs. The REIT only receives the rent for transferring the land and the buildings. This business model guarantees a stable and predictable cash flow for the shareholders. The rental contracts are concluded on average with a ten-year contract period.

Name:	CorEnergy Infrastructure Trust Inc.
Ticker:	CORR
Sector:	Pipelines Gas-Terminals

Market Capitalization:	0.11 billion USD
Dividend Yield:	2.57%
Payout-Ratio:	45.45%

Country of Origin:	USA
Core countries of investments:	USA

Stability ✓
Diversification ✓
Yield ✓

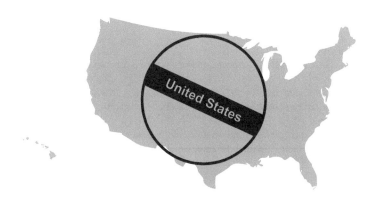

Leverage Ratio: 36%

Sources

56 American Tower Corp.:
https://americantower.com/company/
https://www.finanzen.net/aktien/american_tower-aktie
https://seekingalpha.com/symbol/AMT/dividends/scorecard?s=amt

57 SBA Communications Corp.:
https://www.sbasite.com/English/company/about-sba/default.aspx
https://www.finanzen.net/aktien/sba_communications_reit-aktie
https://seekingalpha.com/symbol/SBAC/dividends/scorecard?s=sbac

58 Uniti Group Inc.:
https://uniti.com/about
https://seekingalpha.com/article/4124787-uniti-unit-presents-nareit-reitworld-2017-conference-slideshow
https://uniti.com/fiber/fiber-services
https://www.finanzen.net/aktien/uniti_group-aktie
https://seekingalpha.com/symbol/UNIT/dividends/scorecard?s=unit

59 Crown Castle International Corp.:
https://seekingalpha.com/article/4307176-crown-castle-cci-investor-presentation-slideshow
https://investor.crowncastle.com/static-files/e2d9530c-7a09-4247-8e63-449ea2bc3926
https://seekingalpha.com/article/4241756-crown-castle-billionaire-bill-gates-quietly-buying-top-dividend-stock
https://www.finanzen.net/aktien/crown_castle_international_a_2-aktie
https://seekingalpha.com/symbol/CCI/dividends/scorecard?s=cci

60 CorEnergy Infrastructure Trust Inc.:
https://corenergy.reit/strategy/
https://corenergy.reit/assets/
https://www.finanzen.net/aktien/corenergy_infrastructure_trust-aktie
https://seekingalpha.com/symbol/CORR/dividends/scorecard?s=corr
https://www.kiplinger.com/slideshow/investing/T044-S001-10-unusual-reits-to-buy-for-high-yields/index.html

61 Getty Realty Corp.:
http://www.gettyrealty.com/about/
https://www.finanzen.net/aktien/getty_realty-aktie
https://seekingalpha.com/symbol/GTY/dividends/scorecard?s=gty

4.12 Entertainment

Entertainment REITs include all types of buildings and properties used for entertainment.

This can include very specialized REITs for casinos or cinemas, but also broadly diversified ones for amusement parks, ski areas or concert halls. In contrast to classic hotel REITs, holiday areas with a special entertainment factor can also be counted among entertainment REITs.

Real estate used for leisure activities can often protect itself well from competition, since its construction has high entry barriers and a region can only accommodate a certain number of facilities of one type. For example, it is not possible to set up as many leisure parks or cinemas in a city.

Risks arise primarily from the income situation of end customers. Especially in economic crises, customers first save on leisure activities. Vacation, gambling, cinema or entertainment are saved to use the little money left over for more important everyday needs.

But crowding out by completely different types of entertainment can also lead to risks. There is a noticeable shift away from cinemas to home streaming services. New types of entertainment such as Television, video gaming, virtual reality lead to a change in user behavior so the buildings of the REITs will experience weaker demand in the future.

EPR Properties[62]

EPR is a REIT that specializes in buildings for the entertainment industry. Its portfolio includes 367 leisure facilities in 43 United States and Canada.

His investments are broadly spread across several categories of the entertainment industry. They include bowling centers, cinemas, casinos, amusement parks, water parks, marinas, golf and ski resorts and holiday resorts. Investments were also made in museums, zoos, aquariums and private schools.

EPR receives additional income from concert revenues and, more recently, from the e-gaming sector.

In its leisure facilities, the REIT also operates and rents out holiday apartments for the duration of its customers' stay.

The facilities are operated by 200 external tenants, who have the necessary know-how and are often large corporations, such as Six-Flags, a large chain for amusement parks.

Name:	EPR Properties
Ticker:	EPR
Sector:	Amusement Parks
	Casinos
	Resorts
Market Capitalization:	2.43 billion USD
Dividend Yield:	-
Payout-Ratio:	-
Country of Origin:	USA
Core countries of	USA
investments:	Canada

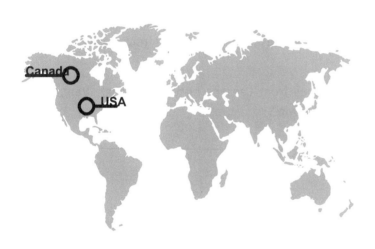

Leverage Ratio: 59%

Vici Properties Inc.[63]

Vici Properties is a spin-off of the casino chain Caesars Entertainment. The REIT has 22 casinos and 4 golf courses as well as other hotels with 14,800 rooms and two racecourses. There are 150 restaurants, bars and nightclubs in its facilities and over 1,600 concerts or live shows take place each year. All investments are in the United States, but not exclusively in the gaming metropolis of Las Vegas.

The majority of the casinos are rented to the former mother of Caesars. Among other things, the Caesars Palace in Las Vegas and the Caesars in Atlantic City. The portfolio also includes other famous casino brands, e.g., several "Harrah's" casinos across the US, several "Horseshoe" casinos, and a hard rock casino in Cincinnati.

The name "Vici" comes from Caesar's historical saying, "Veni, Vidi, Vici" and means "I win".

Name:	Vici Properties Inc.
Ticker:	VICI
Sector:	Casinos

Market Capitalization:	9.37 billion USD
Dividend Yield:	5.80%
Payout-Ratio:	95.37%

Country of Origin:	USA
Core countries of investments:	USA

Leverage Ratio: 48%

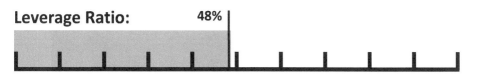

MGM Growth Properties LLC.[64]

MGM is a casino REIT that invests in large and exclusive casinos and resorts. The REIT is a spin-off of the famous MGM Grand casino chain.

He owns 13 properties, which include 27,442 hotel rooms, 1.2 million sf of casino space and 2.7 million sf of exhibition space. There are also 150 shops, 300 restaurants and bars and 20 theater or concert halls in its buildings.

Its brand universe includes some of the most famous casinos in the world, including the Mirage, Mandalay Bay, Luxor, Monte Carlo, Excalibur and MGM Grand.

All properties are in the United States. There they are in cities like Las Vegas or Atlantic City, which have a strong gaming industry. MGM is also active in other cities that are re-legalizing gambling.

Name:	MGM Growth Properties LLC.
Ticker:	MGP
Sector:	Casinos

Market Capitalization:	8.78 billion USD
Dividend Yield:	7.41%
Payout-Ratio:	93.13%

Country of Origin:	USA
Core countries of investments:	USA

Leverage Ratio: 40%

Sources

62 EPR Properties:
https://www.eprkc.com/who-we-are/about-epr/
https://www.eprkc.com/portfolio/portfolio-overview/
https://www.finanzen.net/aktien/epr_properties-aktie
https://seekingalpha.com/symbol/EPR/dividends/scorecard?s=epr

63 Vici Properties Inc.:
https://viciproperties.com/properties/
https://viciproperties.com/about-us-vici-properties/
https://www.finanzen.net/aktien/vici_properties-aktie
https://seekingalpha.com/symbol/VICI/dividends/scorecard?s=vici

64 MGM Growth Properties LLC.:
https://www.mgmgrowthproperties.com/about-us/our-company/default.aspx
https://www.finanzen.net/aktien/mgm_growth_properties_llc_(a)-aktie
https://seekingalpha.com/symbol/MGP/dividends/scorecard?s=mgp
https://www.mgmgrowthproperties.com/home/default.aspx
https://www.forbes.com/sites/brettowens/2018/09/24/5-reit-dividends-you-could-retire-on-forever/#12c9a7842f2e

4.13 Other

The category "other" summarizes all types of REITs whose business model is so special it cannot be assigned to any of the other categories.

Diversified REITs are also listed. So REITs spread over several categories and also cannot be clearly assigned to a single category.

While REITs of the individual categories can often be compared in size, business model or based on their financial indicators, this is not possible with REITs of the "other" category that are not very similar.

W.P. Carey Inc.[65]

W. P. Carey is a mixed REIT specializing in triple net contracts. His investments are broadly diversified across office buildings, warehouses, factory buildings, retail spaces and self-storage. Through NNN contracts, the REIT has little to do with the operation and maintenance of the buildings and only receives a stable rent. Almost all leases have contractually regulated rent increases. 62% of these provide for inflation-related rent increases and thus represent automatic inflation protection.

65.4% of the property is in the United States. Other core markets are in Europe and Japan. Overall, the REIT is invested in 17 countries. Its portfolio includes 1,204 properties that are rented to 324 tenants.

The company was one of the first to enter into sale-and-lease-back agreements with previous property owners to access buildings for the property portfolio. For example, in 2009, 21 floors from the New York Times Building were bought by the New York Times and rented back to them for 15 years. With this process, sellers can use freed up liquidity for the actual business operations and streamline their balance sheet.

Name:	W.P. Carey Inc.
Ticker:	WPC
Sector:	Diversified

Market Capitalization:	11.73 billion USD
Dividend Yield:	6.32%
Payout-Ratio:	89.40%

Country of Origin:	USA
Core countries of investments:	USA
	Europa
	Japan

Stability ✓
Diversification ✓
Yield ⌄

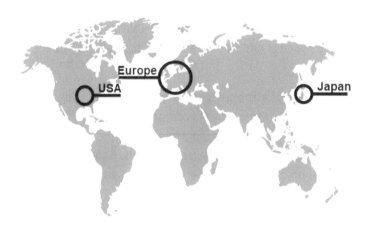

Leverage Ratio: 52%

Safehold Inc.[66]

Safehold is a REIT that specializes in the ground lease process. The REIT owns the land on which buildings are built, but the buildings themselves do not belong to it. The REIT acquires the land under existing buildings by the property owner outsourcing them, thus saving part of his one-off costs when purchasing them. The building owner thereby reduces his interest payments and interest risks. The REIT, on the other hand, receives very precisely and stably calculated income from the lease. The rental contracts are usually very long and have fixed terms for rent increases. Since building owners cannot change locations, both sides are interested in long-term and predictable contract terms.

Safehold is the first and so far the only REIT that specializes in the ground lease process and has established itself as a pioneer in this field.

In contrast to buildings, a property does not lose value due to wear and tear. Ground lease contracts can, therefore, be offered at any point in the life cycle of a property. In principle, all types of property types can be used for ground leases. Safehold has focused on hotels, offices and apartment buildings, targeting the top 30 markets worldwide. He is represented in 20 of these cities.

The largest shareholder is the parent company iStar Inc., a $ 40 billion real estate finance company.

Name:	Safehold Inc.
Ticker:	SAFE
Sector:	Ground-Lease

Market Capitalization:	2.74 billion USD
Dividend Yield:	1.21%
Payout-Ratio:	44.67%

Country of Origin:	USA
Core countries of investments:	USA

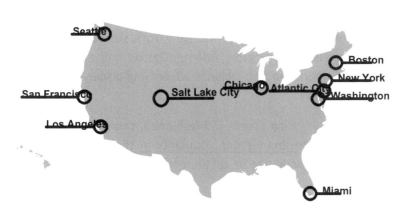

Leverage Ratio: 58%

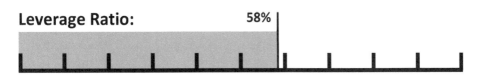

Outfront Media Inc.[67]

Outfront Media is one of the largest owners of advertising media. The REIT operates billboards in and on buildings and streets, bus stops and subway stations, and bus advertising in the United States and Canada. In total, it has over 500,000 displays.

Outfront Media has had many owners in the past, mainly media companies such as CBS or Viacom. Due to the diverse owners, however, more individual advertising operators were consolidated, which enabled Outfront to achieve the size necessary to become a dominant player nationwide.

The REIT operates the billboards in the New York subway, as well as in Los Angeles, Washington, Atlanta, Detroit and many Canadian cities. His portfolio also includes advertising displays in Times Square, New York.

Although banner advertising seems old-fashioned, this form of advertising continues to enjoy great popularity in the USA, so large tech companies also like to be customers of Outfront.

Outfront installs its advertising on land owned by over 17,000 owners of houses, land or public transportation. The latest displays in public spaces are even equipped with WiFi to generate additional income through this service.

Name:	Outfront Media inc.
Ticker:	OUT
Sector:	Advertising Billboards

Market Capitalization:	1.95 billion USD
Dividend Yield:	11.28%
Payout-Ratio:	157.38%

Country of Origin:	USA
Core countries of investments:	USA

Stability
Diversification ✓
Yield ✓

Leverage Ratio: 82%

Lamar Advertising Corp.[68]

Lamar Advertising is a REIT for outdoor advertising, billboards, signs, and billboards in the United States and Canada. The REIT has 200 of its own properties and has installed 360,000 displays - including on third-party houses and at highways and airports. He also runs the side advertising of buses in the street scene. The portfolio includes 3,600 digital billboards that can display moving advertising images like a television.

As a rule, Lamar owns the billboards, but not the country on which they stand. Lamar rents the land or rights to use roof areas from homeowners on whose houses or land the advertising banners are installed.

Lamar bears all costs and insurance risks. This business model does not result in a financial disadvantage for a property owner through a contract with Lamar. This makes it easy for the REIT to find locations for its advertising banners.

Name:	Lamar Advertising Corp.
Ticker:	LAMR
Sector:	Advertising Billboards

Market Capitalization:	6.51 billion USD
Dividend Yield:	5.29%
Payout-Ratio:	143.15%

Country of Origin:	USA
Core countries of investments:	USA Canada

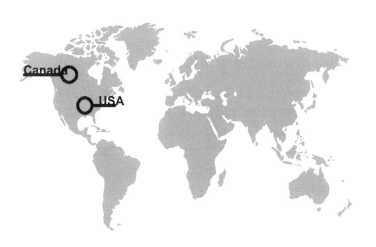

Leverage Ratio: 82%

Landmark Infrastructure Partners L.P.[69]

Landmark Infrastructure is not a REIT, but an L.P., a limited partnership. However, this is the only investment that holds shares in the Landmark Infrastructure REIT. The tax relief and all advantages of the REIT, therefore, apply indirectly to the shareholders of L.P. Depending on the country of origin and tax regime. However, the L.P. Draw disadvantages compared to direct REIT investments.

Landmark Infrastructure is a real estate company that only owns land. The company holds 2,011 properties across the United States and in Australia, Great Britain and Canada, on which radio masts, advertising banners as well as solar and wind farms are erected. The respective infrastructure does not belong to the company, but is owned by the tenant of the property.

The tenants of the properties include large mobile phone companies or energy providers such as AT&T or Verizon. But REITs mentioned in this book, which specialize in radio masts or banner advertising, are also customers. Landmark Infrastructure's REITs American Tower, Crown Castle, Outfront Media and Lamar Advertising are among its largest customers.

All properties are rented using the NNN method. Since there are practically no maintenance costs due to this procedure, the company achieves an operating margin of 97% on sales.

With 5G growth, Landmark Infrastructure continues to benefit from the importance of its locations.

Name:	Landmark Infrastructure Partners L.P.
Ticker:	LMRK
Sector:	Ground-Lease

Market Capitalization:	0.25 billion USD
Dividend Yield:	8.21%
Payout-Ratio:	-

Country of Origin:	USA
Core countries of investments:	USA
	UK, Australia, Canada

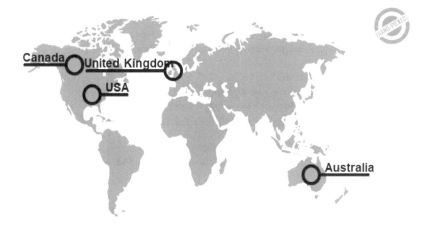

Leverage Ratio: 59%

Equity-REITs
Other

Sources

65 W.P. Carey Inc.:
https://www.wpcarey.com/About-Us
https://www.wpcarey.com/Portfolio
https://www.finanzen.net/aktien/wp_carey-aktie
https://seekingalpha.com/symbol/WPC/dividends/scorecard?s=wpc

66 Safehold Inc.:
https://www.safeholdinc.com/about
https://www.finanzen.net/aktien/safehold-aktie
https://seekingalpha.com/symbol/SAFE/dividends/scorecard?s=safe

67 Outfront Media Inc.:
https://www.outfrontmedia.com/aboutus
https://seekingalpha.com/symbol/OUT/dividends/scorecard?s=out

68 Lamar Advertising Co.:
http://www.lamar.com/About
http://www.lamar.com/InventoryBrowser
https://www.finanzen.net/aktien/lamar_advertising_company_(a)-aktie
https://seekingalpha.com/symbol/LAMR/dividends/scorecard?s=lamr

69 Landmark Infrastructure Partners L.P.:
http://www.landmarkmlp.com/Home/About?Length=4
http://www.landmarkmlp.com/Home/WirelessCommunicationAssets
https://www.finanzen.net/aktien/landmark_infrastructure_partners_lp_partnership_uni
ts-aktie
https://seekingalpha.com/symbol/LMRK/dividends/scorecard?s=lmrk
http://investor.landmarkmlp.com/static-files/f7584d06-fc94-4dac-94c0-589ae0c2327c

5 Mortgage-REITs[70]

In contrast to equity REITs, mortgage REITs, also known as mREITs, do not invest in real values, but in securities based on real estate. "Mortgage" is the English word for a mortgage and is used to secure the mortgage REITs.

Basically, mortgage REITs invest in home loans and have a business model similar to that of a bank. However, they are subject to less regulation than a bank and can also use a different refinancing structure. This enables significantly higher profitability but also shows significantly higher risks and fluctuations.

Mortgage REITs cannot be compared to safe and stable equity REITs. They only have the same name "REIT" because of their tax exemption and their focus on real estate investments.

Mortgage REITs buy packages of loans called mortgage-backed securities (MBS). They bundle a large number of loans from private households that are secured with mortgages on the financed real estate. If the borrower cannot pay his loan installment, the loan can be repaid by foreclosure.

In addition, many MBS are guaranteed by so-called agencies. Agencies are semi-governmental institutions that guarantee the repayment of loans in the event of a loan default. One speaks then of Agency-MBS.

The risk of mortgage REITs, therefore, lies less in the customer's default on credit, but in the risk of changes in interest rates.

Loans to private households are usually concluded with long terms, because a family can usually not pay off a property in a few years. Maturities of up to 30 years are often agreed.

Mortgage REITs buy these loans from lending banks and refinance through loans that borrow them more cheaply. To get cheaper loans, an mREIT chooses shorter terms, sometimes even monthly. Such a strategy is called term transformation. The REIT earns from the difference between the long-term contracts for which it receives interest and the short-term loans for which it has to pay interest.

Since mREITs often work with very little equity and a lot of borrowed money, their leverage increases and they can earn a lot of money even from small interest rate differentials.

However, this construct also involves an extremely high risk. If the interest rates at which the mREIT has to refinance rise, the interest rate differential it deserves decreases. However, if these interest rates rise unexpectedly, it can happen that the mREIT has to pay higher interest than it deserves. Here, there is a loss, which can endanger the existence of an mREIT due to the high level of debt.

To avoid this, mREITs often hedge against the risk of changes in interest rates. This is then called "hedging". However, hedging costs money and, therefore, affects the return. In good times, it is tempting to increase the unsecured portion - but the risk should not be underestimated.

Good management recognizes impending interest rate changes early on and hedges them against them. It finds a well-considered compromise between security and return. So you should be careful with mREITs with extremely high profits because this could change quickly if interest rates rise.

For mREITs to be exempt from tax, they must also distribute most of their profits. However, since their profits do not come from predictable rents, they fluctuate depending on the achievable interest rate differential. Depending on the interest rate environment and financing structure, these fluctuations can be very strong. Accordingly, the dividends paid are subject to significant fluctuations.

In the 2008/09 financial crisis, mREITs had to bear the highest losses of all equity investments. It was their business model that contributed to the crisis when a blown-up financial system believed itself to be deceptive mortgage security and speculated with high levers. The security of mortgages burst when the value of the financed real estate fell sharply. Even the agencies' guarantees could not cover all of the loans on this scale, which led to many bankruptcies and ultimately to the nationalization of the agencies Fannie Mae, Freddy Mac and Ginny Mae.

You should always keep this course of the financial crisis in mind when considering the high dividend yields of Mortgage REITs.

Annaly Capital Management Inc.[71]

Annaly is a mortgage REIT that invests in agency MBS. Most of his investments are loans that are secured with mortgages on residential real estate from private households. Agency MBS are also guaranteed by semi-governmental agencies such as Fannie Mae, Freddie Mac or Ginnie Mae. These institutions act in the event of insolvency of the debtor. Investments in this highly liquid category comprise approximately 77% of the entire portfolio. The portfolio mainly comprises loans with a term of up to 30 years and fixed interest rates and is widely spread across various credit ratings. Smaller parts of the portfolio include short-term or variable loans as well as commercial mortgages.

Annaly is the largest mortgage REIT in the United States by market cap. He has assets of $ 133 billion on his balance sheet. This contrasts with equity of over USD 15 billion. As of December 31, 2019, Annaly worked with a leverage lever of 7.7 and hedged approx. 73% of its portfolio against changes in interest rates.

Annaly has existed since 1997 and continued to pay dividends even in the financial crisis. Although this had to be reduced and the price suffered considerably, as with all mortgage REITs, Annaly is one of the REITs that survived the crisis through good management and subsequently grew strongly.

Name:	Annaly Capital Management Inc.
Ticker:	NLY
Sector:	Mortgage-REIT

Market Capitalization:	9.24 billion USD
Dividend Yield:	14.02%
Payout-Ratio:	102.32%

Country of Origin:	USA
Core countries of investments:	USA

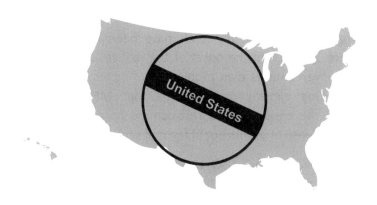

Leverage Ratio: 87%

MFA Financial Inc.[72]

MFA Financial, formerly America First Mortgage Investment, is a mortgage REIT REIT that leverages investments in real estate loans and mortgage-backed securities (MBS). Its main business objective is to generate a profit based on the difference between the interest rates on the investments and the interest expense to be paid.

The REIT invests in agency MBS, MBS without agency guarantee and normal loans. To continue to grow, MFA buys entire security packages, preferably at a discount on the book value, to generate further profits if the borrowers develop positively.

MFA was founded in 1998 and suffered "only" 52% price loss during the financial crisis. The dividends have been reduced significantly since 2006. From the onset of the real crisis, MFA seemed to have overcome its own problems and increased its dividend again. One explanation could be that MFA had foreseen signs of the crisis and had restructured its portfolio years ago at the expense of profits but in favor of security.

MFA's entire portfolio includes USD 13.1 billion in loans. This contrasts with equity of USD 3.4 billion. This capital structure corresponds to a conservative leverage of 3.85.

Based on the history of the carefully managed financial crisis and the cautious leverage, one can expect a conservative and prudent approach at MFA, which has a lower risk compared to other mREITs.

Name:	MFA Financial Inc.
Ticker:	MFA
Sector:	Mortgage-REIT

Market Capitalization:	1.08 billion USD
Dividend Yield:	-
Payout-Ratio:	-

Country of Origin:	USA
Core countries of investments:	USA

Stability ✓
Diversification ✓
Yield ✓

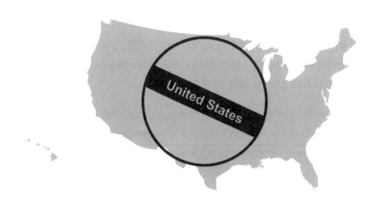

Leverage Ratio: 78%

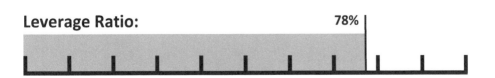

Dynex Capital Inc.[73]

Dynex is a Mortgage REIT and was founded in 1988. During the financial crisis, the share price suffered extremely dramatic price losses and lost almost all of its value. However, he recovered and since then has made significant price gains.

Today's strategy sees broad diversification, conservative management and little leverage as a recipe for success. Management is more of a value preserver than a pursuit of short-term gains. The portfolio includes a larger concentration of short-term MBS contracts. Although this structure has a lower profit margin on refinancing interest rates, it increases protection against interest rate risks.

Dynex invests in both agency and non-agency MBS. 8% of it is invested in commercial MBS, i.e., loans for commercial real estate. The portfolio has a leverage of 9.1.

The REIT is currently struggling with falling dividends and a falling share price due to the interest rate change policy of the FED, but expects cheaper refinancing options again.

Name:	Dynex Capital Inc.
Ticker:	DX
Sector:	Mortgage-REIT

Market Capitalization:	0.32 billion USD
Dividend Yield:	7.64%
Payout-Ratio:	69.54%

Country of Origin:	USA
Core countries of investments:	USA

Stability
Diversification
Yield

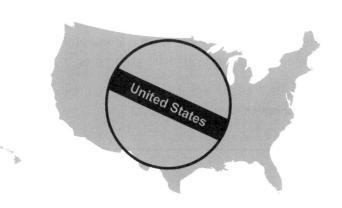

Leverage Ratio: 90%

AGNC Investment Corp.[74]

The mREIT AGNC was founded in 2008 and specialized in agency MBS.

It is a monthly dividend payer and one of the largest mREITs despite its short existence.

The portfolio comprises USD 102.6 billion investments, 88% of which consist of loans with terms of over 30 years. 74% of the portfolio is secured with refinancing of less than 3 months, which results in a high spread on long-term loans, but poses a very high risk of interest rate changes.

The dividend history shows considerable cuts. Since the mREIT was only founded in 2008 and cannot have a long history, it is difficult to estimate how management will handle crises.

Total assets of $ 109.7 billion are offset by $ 10.2 billion in equity. This corresponds to a leverage of 10.72.

Name:	AGNC Investment Corp.
Ticker:	AGNC
Sector:	Mortgage-REIT

Market Capitalization:	7.17 billion USD
Dividend Yield:	11.39%
Payout-Ratio:	69.97%

Country of Origin:	USA
Core countries of investments:	USA

Stability ✓
Diversification ✓
Yield ✓

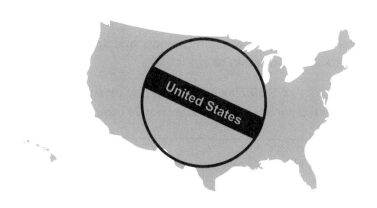

Leverage Ratio: 88%

American Church Mortgage Co.[75]

This mREIT is a mortgage REIT that specializes in mortgages given to American churches. Of the 190 loans granted, 160 churches and other religious non-profit organizations from the USA are creditors. The mREIT has existed since 1987 and finances new buildings, renovations, refinancing or purchases of church buildings.

These tenants can be seen as particularly reliable and fail-safe since they are supported by grants and donations and their payment power is not dependent on economic cycles, as with normal commercial companies. But there is a risk that donations will decrease even in times of crisis.

American Church Mortgage acts as a direct lender and does not purchase loan packages from banks or agencies.

The balance sheet total of $ 39.2 million is offset by equity of $ 10.1 million. This corresponds to a very conservative leverage of 3.88.

Name:	American Church Mortgage Co.
Ticker:	ACMC
Sector:	Mortgage-REIT Loans
Market Capitalization:	2.77 billion USD
Dividend Yield:	16.67%
Payout-Ratio:	396.60%
Country of Origin:	USA
Core countries of investments:	USA

Stability ✓
Diversification ✓
Yield ✓

Leverage Ratio: 71%

Mortgage-REITs
Other

Sources

70 Mortgage REITs:
https://www.edwardjones.com/images/mortgage-reits-high-yield-but-high-risk.pdf
https://seekingalpha.com/article/4252612-risks-remain-prevalent-mortgage-reits
https://www.moneycrashers.com/mortgage-reit-mreit-definition/

71 Annaly Capital Management Inc.:
https://www.annaly.com/about-annaly
https://www.annaly.com/strategy
https://www.annaly.com/~/media/Files/A/Annaly-V2/press-release/q3-2019-investor-presentation.pdf
https://www.finanzen.net/aktien/annaly_capital_management-aktie
https://seekingalpha.com/symbol/NLY/dividends/scorecard?s=nly

72 MFA Financial Inc.:
http://www.mfafinancial.com/IRW/CustomPage/4053645/Index?KeyGenPage=206984
https://seekingalpha.com/symbol/MFA/dividends/history
https://www.finanzen.net/aktien/mfa_financia_b-aktie
https://seekingalpha.com/symbol/MFA/dividends/scorecard?s=mfa

73 Dynex Capital Inc.:
http://www.dynexcapital.com/about-us/mission-and-objectives/default.aspx
http://www.dynexcapital.com/our-strategy/default.aspx
http://s22.q4cdn.com/760998309/files/doc_financials/2019/q3/3Q19-Earnings-Presentation-Final-1.pdf
https://www.finanzen.net/aktien/dynex_capital-aktie
https://seekingalpha.com/symbol/DX/dividends/scorecard?s=dx

74 AGNC Investment Corp.:
https://agnc.com/about-us/
https://agnc.com/funding/
https://seekingalpha.com/symbol/AGNC/balance-sheet
https://www.finanzen.net/aktien/agnc_investment-aktie
https://seekingalpha.com/symbol/AGNC/dividends/scorecard?s=agnc

75 American Church Mortgage Co.:
https://church-loans.squarespace.com/
https://www.sec.gov/Archives/edgar/data/934543/000093454319000072/frm10q093019
https://www.finanzen.net/aktien/american_church_mortgage-aktie
https://seekingalpha.com/symbol/ACMC/dividends/scorecard?s=acmc

6 Disclaimer

This book reflects the information status retrieved on December 1st, 2019. Data, especially the calculation of the dividend yield, can change after publication.

This book provides a first brief introduction to the companies. None of the ideas corresponds to a buy or sell recommendation. As an investor, you make investments on your own responsibility. Further and above all independent research is essential.

No liability is accepted for translation errors - even if they lead to misrepresentation of content.

This book does not constitute legal or tax advice. Liability is excluded in particular for information on legal forms and the tax status of the companies presented. Tax rates and laws can vary from country to country and people can be taxed individually. Please inform yourself independently about which tax obligations apply to you. Withholding taxes may apply in individual countries, particularly in the United States, or tax exemptions for certain legal forms may not be recognized in your home country.

Investments in stocks and real estate are associated with risks. This book is not a recommendation or investment advice, even if certain sentences are formulated in this way. This book is for informational and educational purposes only. No liability can and is not assumed for investment losses, especially price losses.

Disclaimer
Other

Made in United States
Troutdale, OR
10/02/2023

13361373R00116